JENNY WALTON'S

PACKING *for a* WOMAN'S JOURNEY

Jenny Walton's

Packing *for a* Woman's Journey

Nancy Lindemeyer

EDITOR IN CHIEF OF *Victoria Magazine*

ILLUSTRATIONS BY
Alexis Seabrook

CROWN PUBLISHERS, INC.
NEW YORK

Published by Crown Publishers, Inc.,
201 East 50th Street, New York, New York 10022.
Member of the Crown Publishing Group.

Random House, Inc. New York, Toronto, London, Sydney, Auckland
www.randomhouse.com

CROWN and colophon are trademarks of Crown Publishers, Inc.

Printed in the United States of America

Design by Nancy Kenmore

Library of Congress Cataloging-in-Publication Data
Lindemeyer, Nancy
Jenny Walton's packing for a woman's journey/ by Nancy Lindemeyer—1st. ed.
I. Title
PS3562.1511117J4   1998
813' .54—dc21   97-28035
CIP

ISBN 0-517-70662-8

10 9 8 7 6 5 4 3 2 1

First Edition

IN MEMORY
OF MY "*Angel*" GRANDMOTHER,
BERTHA MAUDE KEITHLEY

Acknowledgments

WITH A WORK SUCH AS THIS, EVERY WORD IS AN ACKNOWLEDGMENT of the people in my life who have given me so much to take on my chosen journey. My sister, Lucille Parise, made this book possible with her memories, weaving with mine the tapestry that is both of our lives. She and her late husband, Alfred, have been an ever devoted, if often amazed, cheering section.

Like so many of us, I had put the idea of this collection on the back burner—someday I would tell these tales. Daniel D'Arezzo, my colleague and agent, with optimism and understanding, found the way for me to achieve this volume. I thank him for his particularly sensitive perception of how my story was to be treated. Betty Prashker has been the perfect editor for "Jenny Walton," firm when she needed to be, inspiring and encouraging all the rest of the time. From discussions with Betty, this book took form and became the reality it was sometimes difficult for me, so close, to see.

I have had the support of Hearst Magazines, first from Claeys Bahrenburg, then Cathleen Black, to work on this book along with my duties as editor in chief of *Victoria* magazine. John Mack Carter and Gilbert C. Maurer, instrumental in supporting *Victoria*, have my gratitude for giving me the opportunity of my life without which "Jenny Walton" would probably never have come into being. Mark Miller, also of Hearst, who read an early version of the manuscript, affirmed my belief that grandmothers have a magic place in our lives. My staff at *Victoria* deserves special mention, as does Claire Whitcomb, who edited a number of these essays.

Robert Bennison Lindemeyer and Paul Walton Lindemeyer, my husband and son, both descended from Jenny Walton, are loved beyond belief by her namesake for many reasons but most especially because they are the happiness of my every day.

AMES, IOWA, AND ARDSLEY-ON-HUDSON, NEW YORK

$\mathcal{C}$ontents

JENNY WALTON'S

PACKING *for a* WOMAN'S JOURNEY

Foreword

ON A SPRING MORNING IN MAY 1992, MY HUSBAND AND I ROSE
early. We would soon be driving from our home on the Hudson
River to eastern Pennsylvania, to Cedar Crest College, in
Allentown, where I had once been a student. It was such a beautiful day, we lost our way for a bit, so intoxicated by the benevolent
surroundings that we missed an exit. Blossoms lined our path from
the moment we left.

My husband's mission was to drive me to Allentown; mine was
to deliver an address at the college's 125th commencement. When
we arrived, I donned a gown. (The president told me she did not
wear a cap, so I also chose not to.) At the head of a procession of
some hundred young women, I walked along the center green and
inside the yellow-and-white-striped tent already filled with family
and friends—parents, husbands, little children, undergraduates.
Since January, when Dorothy Blaney, Cedar Crest's president, had
come to my office and asked me to consider the assignment, I had
tried to visualize this day. Now it was here.

I had not graduated from Cedar Crest, but I had been a student
there for my first year and a half of college. My departure had been
some of my doing and some of Cedar Crest's, because I was not particularly happy there. But it had been my first habitation away
from home and, for that reason, it held an important place in my
life. As the years passed, I realized those rolling lawns, trim buildings, and quiet knolls had played their part in the woman I had
become.

After visiting the college that winter, I told Dorothy I would be
happy to give the address. And despite having heard that com-

mencement speakers are necessary evils, I took to heart that I would be talking to young women just beginning their lives, away from this first haven away from home. What I decided to say to them that day is what this book is all about.

My girlhood was not unlike that of many others of my time nor, really, of today. Our clothes are different; but being cared for, accepting that care, and all the while learning what love is about—these are timeless. But there are ways in which my growing up was unusual, not to mention unique.

The singular, devastating event was the death of my mother when I was five. I do not remember her. I know now, being a mother myself, how vital those years are to a child. I have no memory of them whatsoever. Sometimes I wonder if memory has become so important to me because my own earliest memories were obliterated.

My father remarried two years later, and my older sister and I gained not only a stepmother but a new grandmother as well. Bertha Maude Keithley came to live with us when I was seven. Busy lives—my stepmother's, my father's, my ten-years-older sister's—swirled around us. The oldest and the youngest, my grandmother and I grew closer and closer as the years gathered around us.

(That idea of "gathering years"—of time always present, not streaming away and dissipating like the vapor trail of a speeding jet—is a supremely romantic notion. Yet it should not be dismissed as impractical. Time flies or time hangs heavy on one's hands. How we *feel* time is as important as how we understand it or measure it. The years I write about may be gone forever, in one sense, but they inform all the years to come.)

My grandmother and I had an understanding: I was the player, she was the coach. It was she with whom I shared my dreams, it was to her that I went with my hurts and worries. She never seemed tired, cross, uninterested. She was the one who helped me pack my trunk—a big steamer trunk—that bounced along with me when I went off to college. She, most of all, had nourished the dream of college. She, most of all, had given me the confidence to take the first step.

When I returned to Cedar Crest to meet students and imbibe the spirit of a place I had not seen for so long, I could not get out of my mind the image of that trunk packed so lovingly. Hopes, dreams, tears—all were invested in this journey on which I was embarking. Packed in with saddle shoes, plaid skirts, and gray sweaters was my grandmother's wisdom—and, yes, that of all the others who had brought me to that day. That trunk became symbolic, and the theme of my talk followed: "Packing for a Woman's Journey."

I was, briefly, the history teacher my family expected me to be. But for the last quarter century or so, I have been a magazine editor, becoming editor in chief of *Victoria* magazine in 1987. *Victoria* began in two small back rooms at the Hearst Magazine building on Eighth Avenue in New York City. It was certainly one of the most important steps in my own woman's journey, and it provided me with a unique opportunity. In addition to conceiving *Victoria*, I also created a persona for myself from which I could speak to readers from my heart, without the aura (or onus) of an editor in chief. (This persona also beefed up *Victoria*'s small staff in those embryonic days. It was convenient having a writer who never needed direction and never missed a deadline.) As *Victoria* grew, so did the contributions from Jenny Walton—the name I chose to use in my special discourses.

Jenny Walton is, literally, a familiar name. Before our son was born, my husband and I went through that eternal exercise nearly all parents endure. After I had rejected Mavis, and he Søren (thank God!), we settled, with my wholehearted concurrence, on names from his family. Paul Walton for a boy, Jenny Walton for a girl. Jenny Walton, my husband's great-grandmother's name, has never been used except in my columns for *Victoria*.

And so Jenny Walton is the daughter I never had. Her stories, as you will read here, are not exactly autobiographical. It was never my intention to write my life's story. Jenny writes from reflected memory; she writes to see the way best to go; she writes of growing as a woman and of the power of love. Her hand is often guided by her grandmother's, but not by hers alone, because in that trunk that Jenny packs and unpacks so carefully are the affection and goodwill of many kindred souls. Those who teach us to love, those who carry their lamps ahead of us, are the heroes and heroines in our lives.

Not long ago a new member of *Victoria*'s staff, now grown somewhat larger than it was at the beginning, attended a party to which all our contributors are invited. At the end of the party, she asked a longtime *Victoria* staffer whether Jenny Walton would be coming, because she had always wanted to meet her. Her innocent remark met with peals of laughter from that table; but I could have no nicer present than her admission that Jenny was her favorite *Victoria* writer. She now knows, as do you, that "Jenny Walton" is the best I have to remember and to pass along.

I hope she inspires you, as I have so often been inspired, to live with pride in a woman's journey, and to take with you all that is good, kind, graceful, generous, and beautiful, despite the vagaries of time and place.

Where

MEMORY

Begins

Abraham Lincoln's remark that all he was or ever hoped to be he owed to his "angel" mother is open to interpretation. Some say he was referring to Sarah Bush Johnston, the kind and affectionate stepmother who raised him. Others believe the angel was indeed Nancy Hanks Lincoln, the mother he had lost. In truth, both mothers made him the man who lives in our national heart for his fairness, courage, and eloquence. Because my mother died when I was too young to know her, my childhood was not unhappy. At least, I don't think of it that way. I was cared for and loved by women who were my "angels." No mother could ask more for her child.

My Sister's Stories

*For there is no friend like a sister
In calm or stormy weather;
To cheer one on the tedious way,
To fetch one if one goes astray,
To lift one if one totters down,
To strengthen whilst one stands.*

—Christina Rossetti,
"Goblin Market"

Ten years separate us. Not many years, now that we are mature women, our children clustered together in age. But then a fifteen-year-old girl was the grown-up; the five-year-old, the baby sister.

My sister tells me she thinks of me as her baby still, which always makes me smile and sometimes also makes me cry. I think of what a responsibility I must have been in those months and years before and after our mother died. Before she had a girlhood of her own, she was already a little mother in many ways. It was to be several years before my father remarried and brought two new women into our lives. Until then, with the help of aunts and friends, she was my world.

When I was three, I followed her to school so often that I was allowed to join the kindergarten class. That is one of my sister's stories, for I do not remember. Our mother was not well for many years before her death, and even then I suppose I attached myself to my sister's strength. I came to love school from those days on, perhaps because schoolrooms provided the order and safety I needed. My sister tells me that I was, in her words, "very smart" and learned to read at this young age, with the two of us spending countless uninterrupted hours together sprawled on the floor or at library tables with books. One summer, right after my father and stepmother were married, my sister and I were sent for the summer to live with our new stepgrandmother. We traveled on the train from Connecticut to North Carolina under the watchful eye of conductors and, my sister tells me, young soldiers who made sure there were seats for us to stretch out and sleep on. That summer I remember the trips to the library every day and then to the park to read.

I love these stories, these little details of my life. Before home movies, videos, and recordings, all any of us have are those little black-and-white photographs with pinked edges and the not-so-perfect recollections of those who grew up with us. But the stories I love most are the little remembrances of my mother that my sister can bear to share. How painful for a girl growing to a young woman to lose a mother. None of us need know a better expression of such sadness than the hymn that begins "Sometimes I feel like a motherless child."

For me, in some ways, God was merciful, because I do not remember the grief. I only know the emptiness or insecurity I could never quite articulate. A counselor once told me that I took an eraser and wiped clean the blackboard of those years. I think a higher power than my little hand did.

My sister tells me of our mother's tenderness, how she ironed our sheets at night to make sure our beds were warm and welcoming when she tucked us in. She tells of our mother's delight as our father (whom I knew for most of my life as, if not distant, guardedly affectionate) carried me giggling astride his shoulders. My father was a handsome man, tall, with broad shoulders and massive hands. One of my nephews, who is very like my father, has a daughter; and watching him with her when she was tiny, I marveled at the tenderness and delicacy of such a big man. One of my mother's last gestures for her girls was to send my sister shopping for simple red, white, and blue cotton dresses she had seen advertised. I have one of those small photographs of the two of us in those simple frocks, my sister's arm holding me tightly around my shoulders. My dress has an American flag appliquéd on as a pocket; my sister's waistband reads, "Made in the U.S.A." Looking at the picture on my mantel among other photos of family and friends, I hardly recognize us. My sister, with her long neck and graceful good looks, and I radiate such haunting innocence. It tells a poignant chapter in our family's history: my mother too ill to leave her home; my sister, her messenger, helping her care for her daughters.

What I cling to about my sister's stories is that she alone can remember the magnitude of our mother's love. No one else could give me that. No one but her daughter could ever understand Mama. I have felt my mother's hand as she dressed me in her impeccably ironed and starched dresses because my sister has told me. And her memory is perfect.

My sister had four children of her own. Three are with us still, and they know that her role as a mother began long before they were born. Her baby sister was her precious charge, and she protected me as she was to protect them. Her young wisdom never failed her, and our mother would be proud.

An Old Queen Anne House

At one time the house in which I grew up sheltered a large aquarium of tropical fish, two surly cats, a persnickety canary named Michelangelo, a dime-store turtle, and a fallen-from-grace Scottie named Chips. There was room for all of us, too, in the old Queen Anne at 1055 Stratford Avenue on the corner of Fifth Street. We moved into this roomy Victorian shortly after my father and stepmother were married. I lived there until I went to college. While I was away, our lives changed and a time came when I was never to return to that house again. But in many important ways I live there still, sleeping deep in the mattress as I never have anywhere else.

Like the menagerie we had gathered, we were individuals who were not yet a family when we first climbed the stairs of the rambling old porch and opened the large oak door with the stained-glass window. Like the house, to whom time had ceased to be kind, the window was a mixture of dull colors. But from that time on, it was to shine like a jewel as long as we resided there. It would take great effort to turn this aged relic into a warm, comfortable, and welcoming place; it would take goodwill and love to make a new family. My sister and I had, just months before on a May morning, stood beside our stepmother as she married our father in a quiet ceremony in a pretty little chapel. I remember how lovely she looked in a fitted suit with exquisite beading around the bodice, a white orchid pinned to her shoulder. My father's new wife told us, "You are never to call me Mother, because I never want you to forget that you had a mother of your own." That was her style (we called her by her first name, as she had requested), and her excellent taste extended to our home. She was small but hardly frail, and she had been quite a horse-woman, deciding to give up riding when a friend suffered a fatal accident. I am especially fond of the pictures of her in her riding habit. She stands with soft waves about her pretty face, her legs just a bit apart—the touch of defiance I was to come to know well.

While my stepmother was to be my touchstone of femininity, she was also the strongest woman I have ever known. Her soft silk dresses, furs, gloves, and perfume aside, she was to me something of a general. She organized our lives, my sister's and mine, and we respected her completely. She and I were to have our soft moments, like the times I sat by her dressing table as she did her makeup or fixed her hair. She would wear a lovely dressing gown as she performed her rituals. When she was dressed, I watched her select her earrings, and she would give me a smile as she left the room. Her teeth were large for her face, but pearl white, and her smile was often like a merit award; when she was stern, her eyes saw right through me. More than my sister, I found myself on the receiving end of her piercing look, for I was as strong-willed as she. "A clash of wills," my grandmother said, and shook her head.

From the beginning, I did not hesitate to call my step-mother's mother Grandmother. There was no good reason not to, so we fell into it naturally. There were times, when I was older and she was getting very old, that I came up with nick-names to make her feel younger. She sometimes called me "Chicken," and I responded with "Toots" or "Butch." A much taller woman than her daughter, handsome but not beautiful, my grandmother was the soul of benevolence without being a pushover. More and more, she was to run the day-to-day house-keeping, after her daughter had taken the thirteen ramshackle rooms of our house and turned them into an attractive, welcoming home. My stepmother then went out into the community to find her satisfactions in working for church and civic organizations—everyone's number-one volunteer.

Lamenting that houses like the one I grew up in don't exist anymore won't bring them back—and maybe they shouldn't exist anymore. After all, it took two women and two girls to manage this one; we never had outside help. For me, living there was more like being a citizen of a country than just a resident of a house. My room, with the dark mahogany furniture my grandmother had brought with her, was off the landing between the flights of stairs that led to the attic and the kitchen. It had probably been a maid's room at one time, because you could close it off from the other second-floor bedrooms.

I crept down the winding stairs to the kitchen to have breakfast and sometimes camped out on the steps with a book or magazine, next to the crocks where my grandmother's fruitcakes hibernated until Christmas. These she occasionally brought to life with a splash of bourbon, and she also kept her infamous doughnuts there, waiting to spring them on a family conditioned by countless banal, or worse than banal, batches to politely refuse. An incomparable cook, she never mastered even acceptable doughnuts, though she kept trying for perfection. I ate one every once in a while to be kind.

Or I escaped to the attic, where I spent hours on end. "Where does that child go?" my grandmother asked in frustration, probably as she was trying to get me involved in a task or chore. My house conveniently hid me.

What I came to love about that house, and what I have always looked for wherever I have lived, are the places that promise intimacy. And while all of us sought our privacy—my grandmother, in her room with the big mirrored dresser full of her linens and things she hid away, embarrassed when she forgot them, and with the bed I got to stay in when I was recovering from the measles, with its stately paneled headboard; my sister, in her room with her enviable bird's-eye-maple furniture, so ladylike and delicate; and my parents, whose room in the front of the house was the size of our living room, with the bay window where my father sat reading for hours on end—we also had great spaces for togetherness and conviviality. Even I, the kitchen mouse, loved the parlor on Sunday afternoons.

At the heart of the parlor was my stepmother's Baldwin piano; next to it, a table and lamp said to date from Napoleon's time. It made a lovely light as my stepmother played for us after dinner, songs like "Deep Purple" and "Pale Hands." Her fingers rolled across the keys when she launched into her favorite Chopin. Oh, she had great plans for me to become a pianist, too. First she tried to teach me, then she enlisted the help of a sympathetic nun at the local Catholic school, and finally I was turned over to a slightly mad teacher who sat me down while she played for me. I was not to be a pianist, as I was not to be a ballerina dancer; my stepmother kept trying to find just what talent I might have—alas! But I would perch on the front staircase as she played, or wedge myself on the lover's settee in front of the fireplace, listening in rapture. (The settee was the velvet Victorian antique in the shape of an S where our Scottie, Miss Chips Lovendale Tweed, the Third, had disgraced herself, having attacked one of the pillows. "That dog is never to be left in this room alone" was the edict. Of course, no one was willing to enforce the edict, and luckily Miss Chips remembered her distinguished pedigree and sinned no more.) In front of the windows, curtained in heavy lace, as was the entire first floor, my stepmother placed a massive marbletop table covered with framed pictures of the family. Among the hobbies she embraced was photography, and she even printed and hand tinted pictures of my sister and me. She lost interest at some point, so the chronicling was somewhat erratic. There were far too many portraits of me with hair bobbed below my ears and a big bow looking like a sail on my head. I was assigned the dusting of all the painted china and trinkets in the parlor, and to amuse myself, I rearranged them each time. When I became known as an excellent photography stylist, I credited my parlor dusting with encouraging my skills of composition. Our parlor held on to its niceties with a vengeance. I always felt special there, and guests, usually escorted through it on their way to the living room, always seemed to stop for a moment or two as if they were in a museum.

Sliding doors—pocket doors, as they are sometimes called—separated the parlor and the dining room from the place where most of our family life took place. The first Christmas at 1055 those doors were barricades to my curiosity. On Christmas morning, with me standing on the landing across the parlor, the doors were slipped backed into the wall revealing a magic I shall never forget. The decorated tree was trimmed with "a million" shining ornaments, and beneath it lay a surfeit of riches. As I grew older, the doors remained open and streams of visitors came to view my stepmother's village. We were all on our knees at her direction, placing little mirrors as lakes and velvet-clad figures as villagers. A Santa elegantly groomed in a costume trimmed with real fur overlooked the cottage buried in hills of cotton snow. Every year the village grew even more spectacular. And the dollhouse I received when I was ten became an annual display as well. It had been built with real glass windows by a German cabinetmaker. No one ever spoke of it without mentioning these two facts. The ladies of the house furnished it with everything from a miniature silver tea set to tiny paintings in gold frames atop brocade-covered walls. My stepmother, enlisting my sister and grandmother in her zeal, had combed antique shops for months for all the furnishings—and what they couldn't find, they made. After the village, it was the living room's big attraction at Christmastime.

"Those windows are the soul of this old house," my grandmother would say, perhaps justifying her commitment to keeping them sparkling clean. I was to encounter another such fanatic in my husband's aunt Mary, who in her nineties enlisted her devoted nephew in window washing while chores at our own house went begging. We used vinegar to get them gleaming, and after they passed inspection, we rehung the freshly washed and starched lace curtains. My grandmother would get me in the backyard with the curtain stretchers set up and try to make a game of getting the curtains hooked onto every torturous spike. I can feel my fingers tingling now as we both worked feverishly away. When dry, the lace was "stiff as a board," and my grandmother was satisfied that the job had been done right. Hardwood floors you could "see your face in" were another passion, and we waxed and buffed them on our hands and knees.

I have spent a lifetime searching for the sense of that room, trying to duplicate the things I could, like the chintz valances and the soft floral rugs. This is where I can still sit in the big maroon chair with its carved mahogany frame and wait to be told not to curl my legs up under me—"It's not good for your circulation." I hear the tender nagging; I still curl my legs; I still feel uneasy when I do. In this room, I learned to hold the yarn high and at just the right tension as it traveled around my thumbs, my grandmother winding balls for her knitting as we settled in on a Sunday evening. "Child, keep your arms up," she cautioned when my attention began to wander, probably to the radio program we were all listening to. Here she taught me to knit, examining each row for its evenness. Here she told me stories about growing up on the Nebraska prairie, as I hung on every word and her daughter needlepointed away, her attention elsewhere—she had heard it all before many times.

In front of those lace-covered windows, boyfriends sat and pretended to do homework. My father took my first prom picture here, of me in a blue taffeta dress with netting pulled up practically to the tip of my chin while a skinny boy with a white jacket stood next to me, yellow roses in his hand. I am grinning from ear to ear, the junior-class "brain" on her way to the senior prom. Over one eye a wayward wave has slipped, completely covering it. My father thought my stepmother had put one drop too many of perfume behind my ear. "Nonsense," she said, fastening a single row of rhinestones around my neck, her special gift for the occasion. Simplicity was usually her rule with jewelry. All my life I have heard her advice: "If you're in doubt, take it off." The young man helped me slip into a full-length taffeta duster, my grandmother's contribution to the ensemble, and we were out the door past the porch glider where we had talked our way into being the friends we are still.

Our dining room was a crystal palace. My father's father always came at Thanksgiving. A massive man with down-to-earth ways, he looked more than a little awkward sitting facing the crystal chandelier, performing his ritual of carving of the turkey at each of his children's tables. There were at least five such carvings in any one year. Like my father, he had very powerful hands; he sometimes demonstrated his strength to his disbelieving grandchildren by snapping an apple in half before our very eyes.

The prisms of the chandelier replicated the kaleidoscope of our lives in shimmering colors as the summer sun peeked through the lace curtains and set the room aswim in rainbows. Winter meals were lit by candlelight, and those dangling bits of glass we routinely cleaned one by one captured the glow. Displayed everywhere in the room—on top of the sideboard, completely subduing a tea cart—was my stepmother's American cut-glass collection. Grandpa had to cope with turkey dressing being passed in a cut-glass bowl, so the collection was used on special occasions; but mostly it was on display. I used to flick my fingernail at a pitcher or punch bowl now and then to hear them "sing," the hallmark of true leaded crystal, I was told. Pressed glass, which would never have been allowed into our dining room, will not do this. So this was our crystal palace, a place where I would never fling my schoolbooks on the crochet-draped table. My stepmother had made the tablecloth herself. It was one of many pieces she made with her hands, hands that were never still.

No kitchen table was bigger, rounder, sturdier, or more welcoming than ours. My father's political cronies drank coffee there until late in the night; school committees planned fundraisers there; there I did my homework. On the high-backed chairs that surrounded the table, my grandmother dried her homemade noodles on Sunday mornings. My kindly grandmother, who had the softest cheeks, cared for by creaming her face before she went to bed each evening, and the warmest laugh, was commandant of the kitchen. Oh, my stepmother could cook on occasion, and my father would whip up a weekend breakfast; but my grandmother was always at their elbow, for no dish was left dirty for a second, and no used pot or pan given a moment's rest. In that friendly, spotless room, the screen door from the back porch let in the summer's cool evening breeze as my sister and I washed and dried dishes thousands of times and squabbled about whose turn it was to do whatever. When I became a serious student, needing more and more time for studying, the dear girl would wave me off: "Go stick that nose in a book," she would say, winning our grandmother's approval. Both of them finished the dishes with the soft towels my grandmother insisted on making herself. She didn't abide by the ones that left lint on the glasses.

The best food I ever tasted was cooked and served in our kitchen, huge Sunday dinners with leftovers that kept us contented for the entire week. We begged for New England boiled dinners and chicken and noodles, a recipe she learned from her Nebraska mother. My sister and I both regret that we didn't pay more attention, not that it would have mattered that much. My grandmother's cooking came from her heart and soul, and recipes don't tell you how to give generous helpings of both. When I was in college, getting rides most of the time with the same driver, a boy I had known in high school, he raced to get there in time to have my favorite Friday-night dinner, corn fritters and bacon with apple pie for dessert. He knew my grandmother was waiting for us. Order prevailed in her kitchen: Just as the big tree outside the window lost and regained its leaves with the passing seasons, the windows went from wide open but carefully screened to closed tight and covered with steam as tea was being made for dinner. I am setting the table, probably for one or two more than the immediate family, and the big black stove has something wonderful baking in the oven. What could ever be more?

When I think of my grandmother, she is often in this kitchen in her immaculate apron trimmed in rickrack. Behind her square, thick glasses, which sometimes slipped down on her nose when she was in the midst of hoisting steaming dishes about to be served, were eyes that had been damaged by childhood measles—pretty blue eyes that oversaw my upbringing, that oversaw all our lives at 1055, almost around the clock. I never strayed too far from home when I was growing up. I wanted to hold it so tight that it would never leave me. It never has, nor have any of those who worked so well to give me so much to pack away, to nourish me in the years ahead. No wonder I still live there in my deepest thoughts, no wonder this is the place where I still go to feel a hand lovingly tuck me in sheets sun-dried to the scent of a childhood well spent.

My Father's Stories

and nothing quite so least as truth
—i say though hate were why men breathe—
because my father lived his soul
love is the whole and more than all

—E. E. CUMMINGS,
"MY FATHER MOVED THROUGH DOOMS OF LOVE"

Our household was run by women, as four of us outnumbered my dad. I now have the reverse situation, the only woman in a man's world. My father always remained something of a mystery to me, perhaps as I, in my womanliness, perplex my husband and son. My father often did not let us in on what seemed to me his deepest thoughts. Men of his generation didn't, I suppose. What he did give us was his sense of values, by the way he acted and the things he believed in. And as I grew older, he left me to try to understand reasons that were never directly expressed.

Sometimes it has been years later when I would see the whys. I particularly remember his way of not giving us everything we wanted in the way of praise for accomplishments. I am sure he was happy with my school success, but he always reminded me there were greater achievements ahead and that I would do far more important things someday. His message was that I was not to stop growing, not to stop stretching.

"Did you know that Daddy read the Bible seven times?" my older sister asked me recently. I did not, and I asked her what had possessed him. I did not think of him as a particularly devout man. "It was his search for the truth," she answered matter-of-factly.

My father's closeness with me often came through his storytelling, always inspired by historical facts and great figures. I studied history in college, always deep down in my heart believing that it would be a better tale if my father were again my teacher as we sat in the comfortable living-room chairs, where he often discussed philosophy and art with our minister, who rarely saw him on Sunday but who found his way to my father through his reading and that search of his. Sometimes I caught Daddy at the round oak kitchen table where we sat down to steaming mugs of coffee and cocoa. That was the case one blizzardy afternoon when he told me why Napoleon had lost the battle of Russia. His voice was low and his delivery undramatic; but as he spoke, I was transported to the Russia of Tolstoy's *War and Peace* with its valiant Russian soldiers, weary horses, and Empire-waisted women with hair curled tightly above Dresden-painted features. "It was the winter," he said, "the relentless Russian winter, that helped defeat the great French emperor and his conquering army." But there was more.

When the French began their journey deep into that vast and imponderable land, my father explained, they found roads with ruts too far apart to accommodate the wheel base of the French caissons and other vehicles. Napoleon's army was slowed by having to cope with this anomaly of Russian civil engineering. So handicapped, Napoleon was bogged down by the Russian winter and forced to retreat in defeat.

I remember being spellbound by this anecdote, one my history teacher had never heard of. It was the kind of intriguing perspective that drew me more and more into the study of history, and closer and closer to my father. There was a poetry to his storytelling that went beyond the story itself. I think that is why the tales are now interwoven with my personal mythology.

And so my father found his own way to his children. It is still a mystery to me how hearts hear each other, but they do and will.

The Londons Come to Dinner

It was not long after my father's mother died that we received an unusual bequest. How this was arranged has been lost to all our memories, but arranged it was that on a certain Thursday each month Mr. and Mrs. London would come to dinner. They had, as long as anyone could remember, been my grandmother's dinner guests on that appointed night. Now they were ours.

This happened, as I recall, without any particular discussion or any disruption in our routine. There were some wonderful dinners with the Londons; and while it meant a little more effort on my part to behave politely, I thoroughly enjoyed them.

Mrs. London was like the Queen Mother: plumpish, serene, elegant, benevolent, and very well mannered. Mr. London, a solid man who seemed to have accomplished much in the world, had ensconced himself and his wife in a rather stately Tudor stone house, which we visited on occasion. Mrs. London's brother, Graham, lived with them. He was a tweedier sort and carved wooden animals. I still have a dog, his paws stretched out lazily, that Graham carved for me. I have lost a lot of childhood mementos over the years but never that dog. When my son was a child, he broke its tail, but the piece itself is still sturdy, bringing me memories of our times with the Londons.

The Londons and sometimes Graham were often holiday guests as well, and no party would be complete without them. They were indeed the couple who came to dinner and stayed— through most of my growing-up years. I have thought back on this rather odd arrangement and wondered how my parents were selected among all my grandmother's children to be the hosts of choice.

My grandmother must have known that my father was the son who, without skipping a beat, would gladly welcome the Londons to his table. Since they had no children of their own, and no extended family to speak of, their coming to dinner was a way of giving them a sense of belonging to one. Certainly they had the means to hire a cook or eat in any restaurant they chose. But on that Thursday night each month, they were our Mr. and Mrs. London, part of our family tradition.

So I grew up understanding that there are many different kinds of kindness and many different needs. My father was particularly sensitive to how people love to gather at a bountiful table and share not only a meal but camaraderie as well. Over the years, I have met a variety of people around our tables, especially the big round oak one in the kitchen. I wish I had kept a diary of our guests, writing down their conversations and anecdotes. But some—like Sister Catherine and Julie—are forever in my heart. Sister Catherine was an English missionary who visited our church; Julie, an elderly woman who taught me to sprinkle cinnamon and sugar on pie dough to create an incredibly succulent food.

Like the Londons, both of them were always welcomed to dinner, always warmly accepted into our family life.

My father used to say that the friends and sometimes strangers we invited to be with us at Thanksgiving were every bit as important as the turkey and stuffing and cranberry sauce. Anytime I have been away from home on this holiday over the years, I have always found others who received me in this spirit. Is this not the time to be thankful for so many things, open hearts being at the top of the list? And so my paternal grandmother gave us a magnificent bequest in the Londons, for surely that was the beginning of my understanding of the true meaning of hospitality.

Of course, I never knew that my dad was a favorite son. How could I have? He would never have mentioned it, even if he suspected it, and I'm not sure he did. It would be many years after the Londons came to our table that I was to find out in a most touching manner.

My uncle Charlie never said very much. We talked behind his back about how taciturn he was. We kids even tittered about how hard it was to get a word, or even a nod, out of him. He was in his own world, his own strong world with thick, thick walls. Because we knew he preferred to keep his own counsel, we got used to not asking him very much, never being more than ceremonial in our greetings.

But he chose the right time to speak his mind at the time of my father's death. There was one burial plot left in the old cemetery where my grandparents were laid to rest, next to a daughter who had died as a tiny girl and four children, three sons and a daughter, who predeceased my dad. The family held a meeting to decide whether or not my father would be given the privilege of this honored resting place by his parents. As in all families, there were points of intense disagreement. The matter was simple for Uncle Charlie.

"My brother loved our parents more than any of the rest of us," he said in a clear and ringing voice. "He never faltered in his devotion to them; they would want him with them most of all," he said, ending his piece.

Silence fell over everyone; not another word was said. My father rests where he belongs, beside the mother he thought a saint and beside the father who came to our house to break apples in half for us children, amazed at his great strength.

Just the Two of Us

And were an epitaph to be my story
I'd have a short one ready for my own.
I would have written of me on my stone:
I had a lover's quarrel with the world.

"THE LESSON FOR TODAY"

Lines from Frost's "The Lesson for Today" are what I think about on a wintry day when I am out of sorts with the world. They always seem to offer the kind of wisdom my grandmother dispensed when she simply said, "Take heart, Child."

There are times in all our lives when "taking heart" gives us the simple courage to use our good sense and special resources, to count our blessings, to stand tall and get on with it. Life depends on those who get on with it, I have always been told, yet sometimes it doesn't work to trudge ahead wearily. We all need periods of reappraisal and renewal, to take stock and take heart.

Whenever I wonder whether the world is getting better or worse and remember the fears of other generations, it occurs to me that Frost's determination to have a "lover's quarrel with the world" is a very good choice indeed—and an excellent lesson for today. In this way, we affirm our love and renew our commitment to the things that matter most.

At such times, I especially appreciate a beautiful flower—particularly the rose. Whenever I hold one, I fondly recall the wisdom of those two quarrelers, Robert Frost *and* my grandmother.

Bertha Maude Keithley

When I first met my grandmother, she was not as old as I am now but seemed so—even older. Women took to age differently in her time. I have never had her dignity. Maybe it is something we have unknowingly given up in our demand to be forever youthful.

As a Girl Scout, I stood as an honor guard for Eleanor Roosevelt, who must have been around my grandmother's age when she gave a speech in my hometown. It was not her words that have stayed with me all these years, but rather her kindly demeanor. She seemed to me so tall all in black. She wore a hat like an inverted saucer, much like the one my grandmother put on for church. The bend of her body as she shook hands with me, the gentle smile that came across her face when she saw us all lined up in our green uniforms and silly beanies—I felt then that I was touched by magnificence on that stage, and I still do.

In her humble way, my grandmother resembled Mrs. Roosevelt. Though educated in a one-room prairie schoolhouse, she had become an elegant woman—at least, that is how I think of her. Mrs. Roosevelt eschewed the frivolous perquisites of her class; my grandmother never had them. They both knew who they were and were at peace with themselves.

A few years ago, I was very ill, delirious with fever. I sensed my grandmother by my bedside. It was her apron I saw. When I remember her now, she is usually wearing a housedress and apron, ones she made herself and bequeathed to me, a legacy of all the years she took care of me. But when she went to church on Sunday, or when we all went into the city for dinner at a "fancy" restaurant, she always looked lovely. She had very comely legs and was quite slender, actually. Her husband had always complimented her on her figure, she would tell me, smoothing her hands over her hips and turning from side to side before the mirror. One year my parents gave her a fur neckpiece, and she enjoyed wearing it to church and when she went somewhere special. When she put it on, she also wore some of the jewelry her husband had given her. He had died before she came into my life, but she was proud of the crescent moon of diamonds and the solitaire that had been her engagement ring. Her diamond earrings she wore everyday, except when she occasionally exchanged them for ruby studs. Imagine diamond earrings and aprons trimmed with rickrack as a costume for cooking and cleaning.

My grandmother belonged to the Eastern Star, the women's auxiliary of the Masons. For special events at her lodge, she wore evening dresses and silver slippers. She always hoped I would join. I never did, even with the bribe of her onyx and diamond "Star" ring.

She and I shopped for clothes together, and she sewed for my sister and me expertly. She was still making me dresses when I was out of college and "on my own," and knitting me sweaters, although the time came when I made her one, because her hands had become crippled with arthritis. My sister and I still talk of missing the thick flannel nightgowns she sewed for us. You don't find flannel like that anymore, we both agree. Those gowns were the warmest, coziest things ever. When I was in high school, I encouraged her to make me several dresses from flannel, dark prints we had found. They were smashing, and my sister likes to credit me, rather than Laura Ashley, with being the first one to make daytime wear from nightgown flannel!

But it is in those aprons that I often choose to dress her in my remembering. They bespoke her daily work role, a productive role, helping to make a home for all of us. They remind me that her sense of order gave our lives a blessed structure. I have respect for that, even if I don't have the lifestyle any longer to make my days follow one after the other in beautiful logic, the way she did, the way she expected me to. But she would trust me, I think, to do it my way well. Or at least as best I could. That is all any of us can do to keep faith with those whose time has passed.

A Red Coat and a Blue

As surely as my grandmother brewed sulfur and molasses and spooned it into us in the first week of March, she bundled up my older sister and me to go downtown to shop for our spring wardrobes. She was particularly insistent that our coats for Easter Sunday meet her specifications. Our wishes, I recall, were listened to, but there was always one way in which Grandmother prevailed.

My sister was tall and lithe, with hair the shade of beautifully rubbed wood—chestnut, my grandmother called it. My sister's eyes were a blue-green, and her skin English-fair with a dusting of freckles. I, on the other hand, was destined to be shorter, with darker hair and eyes the same deep brown that my son's are now. My grandmother insisted that, given our genetic traits, my sister should have a blue coat and I, a red.

For some reason this spring ritual is very prominent in my memory, even though we made a similar excursion in the fall and those heavier coats were also blue and red—just a deeper shade.

There was one advantage to my grandmother's system. Despite being the younger sister, I was never heir to my sister's coat from the year before, for her color was clearly not right for me. According to my grandmother, these garments, which we grew out of at an alarming rate, were destined for cousins or friends who were selected because they had the appropriate eye and hair colors.

Over the years, my sister became "allergic" to blue and, to this day, refuses to wear it—especially outerwear. I must confess I think her reaction a bit excessive, particularly since I've always felt our grandmother had a way of knowing what was best in most things.

My own little tribute to her taste and determination is to always have at least one red coat in my wardrobe. I do not buy one each season or even each year, but ever in my closet is that bright note to remind me of the loving, caring woman who so dutifully went about the business of raising young ones with such assurance.

Once on a particularly dreary day when I was in college, I was trudging along when one of my professors stopped his car and asked if I would like a ride. I was very pleased at this solicitousness and, once tucked warmly inside, asked how he had recognized me through his foggy car window. "How could I miss you in that red coat!" he retorted. How indeed!

My current red coat is looking somewhat threadbare, so it is time to take myself downtown and shop for another. I look forward to the spring day when I will slip it on, knowing that I am most appropriately dressed and that I definitely look bright enough to be spotted as I walk along the street—perhaps attracting another gracious bit of attention.

Proud as a Peacock

For many of us there is a special family memento that means more than any other because it recalls times we have never forgotten or the true spirit of a loved one. Sometimes all share the same feeling; sometimes it is in one heart alone. An embroidered peacock, a grandmother's true artistry, is that kind of treasure.

When I saw the mysterious peacock for the first time, I must have been about twelve. My grandmother took it from one of the mahogany drawers in her dresser, a place that always yielded interesting things to me.

While I spent those precious years when we were together making the world of books my main horizon, she persisted in teaching me her world—cooking, canning, sewing, knitting, embroidery, housekeeping par excellence, and even carpentry.

My grandmother was born in Nebraska before it was a state, and her frontier upbringing had taught her many lessons. She could do more things well than anyone I have ever known. Her problem with me was that I did not learn the lessons she intended, and when her patience wore thin, she would stop to tell me a story—then do the chore herself.

I never learned to quilt skillfully. My fingers did not glide over the bits and pieces of fabric as hers did. But I remember every detail of the tales of quilting parties in Nebraska that went on into the night—the children put to sleep in barn lofts. And I remember her first dance when her beau arrived late in a horse-drawn sleigh and quilts warmed them both as they took off into the snow.

My grandmother's baking was the best in the neighborhood. I thought, in the world. She made masterpiece cakes for friends all the time. But it was her pink apple pie that was legendary. (Her secret: the addition of little cinnamon candies to the apple mixture.) I shall never forget the sight of pies on every table and chair when I got up to go to school one morning. My grandmother had stayed up all night making more than fifty pies for a dinner at the Methodist church.

She would stay up all night to put the finishing touches on a party dress for me or my sister. A perfectionist, she would rip out seams over and over if the fit was not expert. And since I seldom liked to stand still for all that, I frequently felt a knuckle. The sewing machine was another place where I failed to meet expectations. I never learned to sew well, although, when she gave me a machine when I was married, I did use it as long as it lasted; and because it was her machine, it lasted a good long time.

I did become a good knitter—best in the family, in fact. And I did learn every commonsense saying in the English language. While I never learned to cook the way she did, I learned how to stay up all night for something that mattered—even if apple pies were not the end result. My grandmother taught me to love accomplishment.

The peacock that went back into the drawer that day when I was twelve stayed there for many years. For some reason the exquisite piece she had stitched when she was a young woman was never framed or displayed—now it is in my care. I have always loved it and remain forever proud of the peacock and its creator.

Going Up the Street

Margaret betrayed her Missouri upbringing when she took my arm as we walked along a busy New York street. She did it just the way my grandmother used to when we went "up the street" together. Margaret, a warm and wonderful colleague, must be in her eighties; my grandmother was somewhat younger when the two of us took those strolls. In both cases, the gestures were of spontaneous closeness and affection.

Often my grandmother and I were on our way to the ice-cream parlor on summer evenings when supper had been early and it was still light. Everyone in the neighborhood seemed to be out. We did a little fixing up before we left the house in case we ran into the minister or one of the ladies from the church. We enjoyed our time together so much, though, we weren't looking for anyone else.

My grandmother loved banana splits. I don't think I'd eat one on a bet now, but those sweet creations, made with home-made ice creams and soda-fountain delights like crushed pineapple, were heaven then. A Greek family ran our candy and ice-cream store. Chrome booths and black leather seats told its vintage even then. The tile floor was immaculate, and the large sparkling cases held neat rows of hand-dipped chocolates, which we sometimes took home or bought to have on our Saturday matinee dates. We adored going to the movies together, although it became a bit of an undertaking the time my grandmother decided to try out her new hearing aid at the Majestic.

She could count on me to be part of the experiment. The device was some contraption that hung around her neck, beep-ing at undesirable times. We got through the double feature ducking our heads in embarrassment when the thing misbe-haved. I don't remember if her hearing improved dramatically after that, but the aid didn't make another excursion to the movies.

I must have been in the ten-to-twelve-year-old range when our up-the-street jaunts became a ritual. We went to the dime store together and looked at everything—we even betrayed our Greek confectioners by buying chocolate creams that were really dreadful but lasted us through a double feature. Once, my grandmother left one of her hand-knit mittens on a counter, and just about everyone in the store joined in the hunt. We found it at last.

The truth is, it didn't matter where we were going, we took our time and enjoyed each other. She took my arm and held me close to her. We walked that way together for years on end. I can feel that pull in my heart still. My husband takes my arm just that way sometimes now. It is always unexpected and it always grips me. I take my son's arm for a minute or two and make a few determined strides sometimes, not often. I miss going "up the street" with my grandmother. I always will, but her love and her strength hang on to me wherever I go.

"COME SUNDAY"

I was raised in a rather regimented manner by my stepmother. I have always called her that even after she legally adopted both my sister and me. She gave us endless lists and endless chores and endless rules. Asking for a piece of fruit was required, for example, rather than just helping oneself. Cookies and other treats had the same requirements. Her reasons were valid, especially as I look back. Respect and discipline were certainly part of her plan, as was knowing in a practical way what provisions were on hand and what was not. But on Saturday, after our morning chores, the rules were suspended. The formality of our lives changed dramatically. The refrigerator was stocked with cold meats and tuna salad, all manner of things that we were allowed to help ourselves to as we wished. I loved Saturday for its freedom, for its pure pleasures, like going to the movies and not having to worry about homework. To this day, I wake up on Saturday morning with expectations other days do not offer. I was conditioned to understand that rewards are just that, and not how each day is lived.

Not too long ago I sat in a recital hall and watched and listened as my son played a duet with his teacher. The music was Duke Ellington's beautiful spiritual "Come Sunday," and the sound of my son's sweet tenor saxophone and the precise piano notes struck by Becky, his instructor, took me back to Sundays years before.

Since that recital, I have discovered the words to "Come Sunday," which to me are a hymn to harmonious times, a reminder of the Sundays of my childhood. It is in the garden of my memories I find the scale to judge and appreciate such measured moments.

Sundays in my growing-up years were a paradox. On the one hand, there was an order to the day, almost like a military regimen; but on the other hand, there was also a gentle pace that no other day of the week afforded.

Of course, we were not to lie abed late on Sunday morning. My grandmother was up early in the kitchen, first cooking a respectable before-church breakfast for all of us and then making it perfectly clear we were to finish quickly so she could get on with the preparations for Sunday dinner. She occupied the command post for Sunday meals, and in the way she took charge she might as well have had shoulder boards and stripes on her apron. How many Sunday mornings did I sit at the round oak table and complain that I was not interested in dinner, as I had not yet finished breakfast? She paid me no mind.

Sunday school and then church, just blocks from our house, were next on the day's agenda. I sang in the junior choir, mostly mouthing the words because my musical talent lagged behind my enthusiasm for filing down the main aisle in a crimson robe and white starched collar. I collected medals for perfect attendance. I learned Bible verses, hymns of thanksgiving, and stories about good works. Then I returned home to Sunday dinner.

Before the meal was served, our high-backed kitchen chairs were often the resting places of great circles of noodle dough, chicken and noodles being one of our favorite dinners. As we worked toward the dinner hour, the table would be set and more vegetable dishes than I have seen since would be at the ready. By midafternoon when we sat down together, time seemed to slow to the tempo of a flower blossoming. I never wanted Sunday dinner to end. Though I knew the fate of washing dishes awaited me, that was not the reason for my reluctance. I never wanted to let go of that blessed feeling of a family in accord.

But once the dishes were done, the rest of the day was a delicious eternity with no imperatives. We did various things—visiting, walking in the park, reading the paper. As the afternoon wore on, my stepmother and grandmother gathered their sewing baskets and settled into chairs to knit or crochet, and I invariably curled up with a book. The day that always began with a brisk sense of urgency had by twilight become the exact opposite—a respite, a quiet time to dream.

The strains of "Come Sunday" accompany this memory, and

I will always remember sitting in the recital hall so far away in time and place from my childhood, feeling a communion of spirit with the composer and the musicians. That harmony in my spirit echoes those precious times when I first learned that Sunday is both a taskmaster and a day with no timetables and no cares. To me, the words "Come Sunday" are full of promise.

A First Best Friend

To love me, you must know what hurts me.

—JEWISH PROVERB

Janice Foster and I became friends in the third grade under the kindest of eyes, those of our teacher Anna H. Graham. The first day of school I ran down the newly painted steps of the house on Stratford Avenue and headed "up the street," as my grandmother always said. The summer had gone quickly as our family made our new home, and I had had little time to look for chums. The Babcock family lived just next door, and one of their daughters and I had spent some time together, but we were not to be in the same grade, or even in the same school. At the corner of Sixth Street, I met Janice and we walked together that day— and for the days, months, and years to come.

Our destination was the brick school on the corner of Newfield Avenue. For years Sadie Caldwell had been principal. I already knew Miss Caldwell and her reputation because she was a member of our church, which stood just kitty-corner from the school. Janice and I talked about the strict disciplinarian who ran Lincoln School like an army master sergeant. Janice had already been resident in the drafty old schoolrooms. Tall windows looked across to the friendly little library across the street. The dreaded cloakrooms were dark and inhospitable to the "talkers" who had to spend time incarcerated with the coats and umbrellas.

Perhaps it was because Janice was a three-year veteran of Lincoln School that I bonded with her on that September day. I do not remember what was so special about our original attachment. Our fathers, I was to find out, were boyhood acquaintances. Harry Foster, who was the manager of our local movie house, told me some time later that he and my dad had been "doughnutnappers" in their boyhood days. On their way to school, using long sticks they had whittled to arrowlike points, they would "bag" doughnuts from Mrs. Vinka's Hungarian Bakery, as their succulent prizes cooled in the early-morning hours. We girls were horrified at this confession and smugly always paid for our fresh doughnuts inside, although we both wondered if Mrs. Vinka knew us as the offspring of those naughty boys. A tall, stout woman with her hair pulled back in a bun, she never let on her likely knowledge that several generations of lads had savored forbidden early-morning delicacies at her expense.

Janice and I spent countless hours together in and out of class. When we walked home together, I would often stop in at her apartment, the ground floor of a six-unit building. In that third-grade year, her mother was ill and often in the hospital. I sometimes spent time at her mother's bedside, or at her feet as she rested in a chair in the living room. As the year went on, I stopped in less and less because Janice would say that her mother was too sick to hear our girlish chatter.

The following year, Mrs. Foster died. And Janice and I began to share not only the intimacies of Miss Baker's fourth grade but a grown-up loneliness as well. We never spoke about being "motherless" girls; I came to know only much later that the tragedy of my mother's death enabled me to be of help when someone else suffered that too-great-to-bear loss. But tacitly Janice and I bonded together as never before. No neighborhood birthday party was celebrated or summer picnic enjoyed by one of us without making certain the other was included. When Pat Gillis moved to Sixth Street and became Janice's friend, she became my friend as well. The same was true of my new friends as we progressed through the grades.

I remember Janice as a beautiful girl, and I admired and envied her a little. Her two older brothers, who were already on their own before her mother's death, adored her and showered her with love and attention. One returned from the navy to live with the Fosters for a time, and he spoiled both of us.

As time went on, the walk to school was no longer just to the corner where my church and school lives merged. Our last year was the eighth grade, and we finished in white dresses in the barny old auditorium with Miss Caldwell in tears as she sent us on to the high school, a long walk up hills that seemed to separate us at once from our early school days.

From that June afternoon when Miss Caldwell called my name and I found my way to the stage, astonished to receive the highest academic prize the school awarded, my steps and Janice's steps parted more and more. Going to college had become the singular preoccupation of my young life; Janice was preparing for business courses. We would no longer be sharing classes and teachers. Encouraged by early academic achievement, I studied harder and harder to win the scholarships I would need to go on to college. There were fewer opportunities to take in free movies at Harry Foster's behest.

Our day-to-day sharing diminished, but we remained close, reassuring friends in ways both of us would always value. Over time we lost touch, but as each new school year begins, as September light falls on my face for the first time, I see myself an awkward child with too-long legs heading "up the street" to meet a charming girl with a pug nose and hair brushed into rings of shining curls, both of us hustling off on the brink of a first best friendship. What auspicious steps we took, what an imprint on our lives to come. Janice Foster and I were not alone when we needed each other most, when eight-year-old understanding surpassed all.

THE SISTERS CONSPIRACY

Before I was old enough to attend school by myself, I regularly followed my older sister to her classes, walking along as if I, too, were to be allowed access to the wonderful halls of learning. We lived in a neighborhood where everyone knew everyone else, so I was often permitted to "visit" the school, my persistence triumphing over the more formal rules. It was then that my love affair with the art of teaching began.

More than anything else, what I wanted to be when I grew up was a teacher, inspired as I was by confident, kind women who always knew about mysterious things—like the Golden Road from Samarkand, which was the silk route from Asia to Europe, and the number of apples Farmer Brown had left after selling some, eating some, and giving some away. How eagerly I awaited the time when I would no longer have to peek over other shoulders and could make such discoveries on my own. Naturally, these discoveries began with reading.

Mrs. Graham, my third-grade teacher, took me on my first trip to the Newfield Public Library, just across the street from Lincoln School. We students would walk in a line as straight and silent as a West Point parade.

Our teacher, who was to retire that year, read stories to us, a chapter at a time. And we were allowed to pick out books to take home. For many years after, until I went to college, the Newfield Library was a place where I spent countless after-school hours. Often I was there to work on a book report or a research project; more usually, just to be amidst the novels and history books that fascinated me. The librarian was a source of endless suggestions—of new books just arrived or old favorites I was not to overlook.

Even now, I can close my eyes and return to that childhood sanctuary. And with a moment's reflection, I can hear Mrs. Graham's expressive voice reciting *Hans Brinker, or, The Silver Skates*, my very favorite that year.

I cannot recall if I sent each teacher a valentine throughout those early years; I'm sure I did when I was in the lower grades. Anna H. Graham of the third grade would surely have received a loving one, since she was about to retire the year I was in her class. And I'm certain she gave me a beaming smile, sitting behind her desk piled high with the children's classics she had read to us.

When I graduated from high school and was about to leave for college, I visited Mrs. Graham. She told me stories about my class, and how we were so special to her because we were her last. And from a folder, she produced my book reports from the third grade. She had kept them, she said, because she had seen in me a student with a special regard for reading.

I never saw Mrs. Graham again, although I did write off and on, keeping her posted on my academic career. But whenever I have read aloud, I have always tried to do it with the style and sensitivity of this true teacher.

When I look back on my grade-school education, it is with a sense of awe for the teachers who patrolled those coat closets and black-topped schoolyards and who poked us under desks during air-raid drills and guided us in march two-step for fire drills down steel fire escapes, which I secretly suspected had been erected for the June 14th Flag Day exercises. For these holiday festivities, all the classes gathered in formation on the playground as students proudly appeared on the fire-escape platforms singing patriotic songs. In my case, since I am musically challenged, I was allowed to recite some old poetic chestnut as loud as "the shot heard round the world."

I don't think I realized until years later just how many of my teachers were related to each other (three sets of sisters guided my early learning years), and I wonder if these familial ties made my bond with the school even stronger. All my grade-school teachers had a seasoned maturity; I do not remember any fresh-from-college teachers. Oh no. Lincoln School was definitely a bastion of experience. How remarkable it seems to me now that Miss Rock of the fifth grade turned me over with perfect understanding to her younger sister, Miss Rock of seventh-grade English.

The two Misses Rock were petite women who wore similar hairstyles—tight gray curls—and clothes that were prim and distinguished. What is more, I think they even painted their nails. My youthful reaction was that they were very stylish indeed. And while both were fine teachers, Miss Rock of the fifth grade had a kindlier manner than her sister, as well as a warmer sense of humor. (Perhaps by the time you were in junior high school, you were not supposed to need gentle handling.)

Kindergarten and eighth grade were the province of the Chapin sisters, and I loved them both. I hated the thought of leaving Lincoln School and the second Miss Chapin's company, perhaps as much as Anne of Green Gables detested her departure from Avonlea. Although I would have to forsake my family of teachers, it was their pride in me that gave me the courage to head up to the high school up the hill.

"You are wanted in the principal's office," my American history teacher Miss Morrissey said, beckoning me toward the door. A note had just been delivered to her classroom on an early June day when all the windows stood open to keep her senior students alert. It was hard tending to our lessons when graduation was so close. Most of us had already been accepted to colleges. I walked through locker-lined halls with my heart pounding. My mind raced: Had something happened at home? Why was I summoned?

Mr. McGee held his office door opened for me after I had run the gantlet of his administrative staff. I noticed Miss Larkin, the dean of girls, stretching her neck to see me as I followed him in. Mr. McGee was a huge man—not heavy, just very impressive—and a lock of his thick white hair always seemed to be resting nervously on his forehead. He looked at me through heavily framed glasses and in a serious tone told me that I was to be my class's valedictorian and was to report to the speech teacher for help with my graduation remarks. I don't recall that he said anything else. Maybe I was in such a state that I didn't hear anything beyond the essential facts; but Mr. McGee was not the type to make a fuss over a flibbertigibbet girl in shock over good news. Miss Larkin, on the other hand, waved and smiled at me as I hurried out of the office and back to class. Concentrating on American history was now impossible; Miss Morrissey understood my distraction when I told her the news after class was over.

Miss Morrissey and I had been together in history for only one year; I had been in her sister's Spanish class for four years. Neither had ever married, and they lived together; but they were quite different in appearance. The history Miss Morrissey was the blazer-and-gray-skirt type; the Spanish Miss Morrissey was far more up to date. Both were excellent teachers. At the time, it didn't seem unusual to me that so many sisters had been responsible for my grammar- and high-school educations. In hindsight, these five sisterly pairs seem utterly improbable. But surely the continuity of related teachers made me feel at home at school. It was like being educated by and in a family.

When I got to high school, I had begun to take for granted the sister phenomenon. My English teacher for my junior and senior years and my geometry teacher were sisters, although one had been married and they had different names. I liked them both, but I far preferred English as a subject.

I was to find out that a pair of sisters can be formidable.

Each year at graduation, prizes were given for excellence in individual subjects, and it had been a rule or a tradition that no student receive more than one. Fairness was doubtless the basis for the regulation. But I received both the American history and the Spanish prizes that year because my sister teachers battled for me and neither would yield. I wondered if two unrelated teachers would have been more likely to compromise.

The speech teacher, who was not related to any other teacher, as far as I can recollect, did help me with the valedictory speech. All of the family members that my stepmother and grandmother could strong-arm into attending the ceremonies were in the front row, along with my grammar-school principal, Miss Caldwell, and *her* sister, who went to our church, and several of my grammar-school teachers.

It took hard work to achieve the academic average to become the valedictorian of my class; but, as I recall the faces in that front row, I realize how much more than my share of help and encouragement I had been given. The genuine interest of these women who passed me along one to the other, like a relay baton, must have helped much more than I had imagined. This closely knit community where I lived brought up its young people together. My sister teachers were just another part of the fabric of my life for which I have been forever grateful.

Only my family was in attendance when I walked across the stage at college to receive two awards in American history; but Miss Morrissey was pleased that I had pursued my early interest in that subject. I kept faith with her sister, too, by studying as much Spanish as I could and being asked to join the Spanish honor fraternity. I would never admit to her that the very handsome Spanish professor was one small reason for my attentiveness. I might even have gotten a smile out of Mr. McGee if he could have seen my Phi Beta Kappa key, just like the one that hung from his watch fob. On second thought, I'm not too sure about that. He would simply have expected it from one of his students.

A Christmas Discovery

In this world there are only two tragedies.
One is not getting what one wants,
and the other is getting it.

—Oscar Wilde,
Lady Windermere's Fan

The first birthday present I truly remember receiving was a picture dictionary for children. A big book with manila-colored pages, I adored it. This was my first birthday in our new house with our new family, and Christmas was just a week away. My birthday was not ignored, but it was that year to be a footnote to the unforgettable Christmas when the pocket doors slid back to reveal the tree towering over a fanciful scene, one that would grow with us year after year. Every branch had been showered with tinsel. As I was to learn in succeeding years, this task alone is no mean feat, for my stepmother insisted that each strand be carefully hung; she would never allow a tangled piece of tinsel. Beneath the tree, a surfeit of riches awaited me.

Santa Claus never existed in our house except as a jolly myth. My father believed that children should be told the truth to the

degree it was possible. So Christmas meant that our loved ones had given us these gifts out of their caring hearts. I don't recall missing Santa Claus that year or any one since. My own son sat on Santa's lap at the local department store as a childhood rite of passage. While I was not as fanatical as my father about the legend, I think my son, like most children, went along with the fiction for the rewards that it brought. And not just more presents. It was fun, and everyone was in on the act.

But that Christmas I knew where all the presents came from. My stepmother had shopped for the velvet party dress and the shoes I had begged for after I saw them at Holland's

Department Store. They had little stirrups on the side and squarish toes. Both she and her mother had found a baby doll half my size and conspired to create a wardrobe for her like no other. My grandmother loved red, so my doll was cloaked in red taffeta with black lace trimming on her collar and bonnet. They worked together just as they did a few years later when they collected furnishings for a wondrous dollhouse and made curtains and rugs and hung wallpaper.

As I grew older, the ritual of hiding the tree behind closed doors ended and the trimming was made the major event on my birthday. Because my family felt it would be an imposition on other families to come up with gifts just before the holiday, my birthday celebrations were kept intimate occasions. I always invited one or two close friends to dinner, and the tree trimming brought in neighbors, friends, and family who stopped by to watch the progress and incidentally wish me well. I always had a monstrous cake, no matter how busy my grandmother was with her mincemeat pies or brandied fruitcakes. And she always made me something special to wear during the holidays—luckily, nothing so grand as my doll's lace-trimmed taffeta.

What could be more of a celebration? On my birthday, the whole world is decorated. On my birthday, there are always parties at the office and at friends' houses, and I am never left out. I have never been sorry that I was born on a snowy morning just six days before Christmas. We still try to decorate our tree on my birthday, or begin the process. During our son's college years, we waited until he was home; he didn't want to be left out of the ritual. And even then it worked out fine. We still keep the family tradition of keeping pretty much to ourselves on my birthday, and presents are small and meaningful things. After all, it would be hard to find anything that could surpass the picture dictionary for children I received the year my remembered life began.

My sister began a few years ago sending me flowers from her grandchildren, six now. And this year when we all got together on the Sunday before Christmas, she told them the story of the day I was born with snowdrifts so high that she was almost buried in snow when she stepped off the porch. The little ones' eyes widen; the older ones have heard it all before but don't seem to mind.

Except for bouts of moodiness and a bit of a headstrong nature, I was pretty much an obedient child. My stepmother did have very high standards for how children should behave. Because she arrived at motherhood with children half-grown, I sometimes think she wanted us to be perfect in order to prove that she was doing a good job. My sister and I were not perfect, but our stepmother was doing a good job in many ways.

She was uncanny in detecting miscreant behavior. "Have you been at my dressing table?" she would ask me. How could she possibly know? I thought, my young mind not realizing that powder probably covered the mirrored top. "Yes," I would admit, knowing that I was not supposed to be "messing about her things."

In my ten-year-old cleverness, I discovered the closet where she was stockpiling Christmas presents, and a desire to find out what I was going to get for Christmas burned in my brain. My stepmother, aware that curious children might indeed stage a raid on the closet, had wrapped all the gifts and tied them up with ribbons.

When everyone else was out of the house one afternoon except me and the pets, I had my opportunity. Neither Chips, our usually frisky Scottie, nor the cats, lazing in the sun, seemed to care that I was invading the Christmas closet. With (I thought) preternatural skill, I unwrapped each present, rewrapping it so that no one would discover me. I must have seen some spy movie that encouraged me to fantasize that my mission would go undetected.

The woman who could see a hairpin out of place at twenty paces found me out in an instant. The whole family was stunned. I was mortified and disgraced. My foolishness became my punishment, because I had ruined the surprise of my own Christmas. No punishment could be meted out to match that. As the years went by, the incident brought forth howls of laughter as it was told, and it was, countless times. I still can't imagine what possessed me, but I discovered much more than Christmas gifts in that closet: I learned that the joy of receiving is in far more than the gifts—that when we receive graciously and gladly, we reciprocate the gift with joy and gratitude; and in that moment of shared happiness and understanding, giver and receiver "connect," as E. M. Forster bid us all do.

And I also learned that trying to fool folks doesn't make a lot of sense at any age.

LEARNING TO LOVE
ROCK GARDENS

My father-in-law used to tell the story that he had to learn to swim to graduate from college. He barely made it, and probably

didn't need to be much of a swimmer to publish and edit t..
Strawberry Point *Press-Journal* in northeast Iowa. I knew h..
was rather proud of that accomplishment, because we heard
about it often through the years. Swimming was not to be my
stumbling block to graduation—science was. As it was for James
Thurber, the human eyelash was the only sure thing I could
identify through a microscope. Climbing up to the top floor of
the science building on the campus was like going to the guillo-
tine. I managed to get through botany by gluing myself to my
lab partner and studying like mad. My chemistry professor
wrote equations on the blackboard simultaneously with left and
right hands. That is all I remember about the subject.

When credits were being counted up, it became painfully clear
that I had to take just one more science class—geology was the
only possibility. Rocks, I knew a lot about rocks, I thought. I
certainly had gathered enough of them as a youngster for my
stepmother's rock garden. I hadn't particularly enjoyed the
exercise or the weeding, but at least I could touch a rock—the
frog in biology was an entirely different matter. So I took geology, and I loved every minute of it. For a student of history, it
was just the sort of studying I loved, but without the wars and
personalities. My success with geology also changed my youthful aversion to rock gardening. Just as my father-in-law was
proud of learning to swim, I was drawn to this particular kind of
gardening because I overcame an obstacle.

My first trip to London's Chelsea Flower Show, I wandered
through tents with arbor after arbor laden with roses of majesty
and I walked past every kind of lupine and primrose. But where
did I land for hours? The little alpine gardens where tiny flowering plants and succulents nestled among pretty little rocks.
They recalled those rock gardens of my childhood, along the side

orch of our house, which were continual works-in-progress.

First, of course, rocks were gathered. My stepmother was very clever in getting me and all my friends engaged in hunts and games that ended up with her getting new rocks for her garden. I worried then that my friends were on to her and that invitations to hot dogs and ice cream were merely the prelude to rock hunts. Wherever we went, rocks were sought. Our picnic baskets never came home empty—after fried chicken and pickled eggs vacated, shiny pieces of mica schists and quartz took their place.

Next came collecting plants, often from other gardeners so possessed. The artistry of marrying plant to rock to incline was something my stepmother had a talent for. A little pillow cushioned her knees as she dug around to fit her plants in neatly. She tended her small landscape lovingly and was distraught to see a weed, apoplectic at the trespass of dog or cat. The romance of the garden was then lost on me. I had toted the stones and helped put the garden in, and I was dragooned into maintaining it to immaculate perfection when I would rather have been reading or swimming.

It took me years to realize how my stepmother had passed on her passion for rock gardening. I have never had the desire to create one myself, but I know what it takes to plan, grow, and nurture one—and that makes me an insider. It is a good feeling to understand how one follows a vision; it is a good lesson to have learned long ago on my knees.

AS MY GRANDMOTHER WOULD SAY

"You are like an open-face sandwich—that's what my grandmother would say," I counseled a pretty young coworker recently. She has the softest eyes that tear easily with the slightest emotion. Her generally pure complexion turns a becoming blush when you praise her, and she bobs her head down. She loved the expression and said she had never heard it before. I couldn't imagine; I had heard such phrases all my life.

"You get on that like a duck on a June bug," my grandmother would say to motivate me. Her speech was peppered with such Midwestern wisdom. She also dispensed her commonsense philosophy with every cliché in the English language. "Every dog has its day" was one of her favorite ways to console me when I hadn't had one of my own. She always made little slights much easier to bear, and she usually smoothed my hair or put on the tea kettle in the process of her therapy.

"Sticks and stones" was another one of the phrases she pulled out of her bag of tricks when I suffered a schoolyard slight. Indeed, I was taught to value the bird in my hand and to fear the fire of lying. "Little girl, this too shall pass" got me through thinking that my life was ruined forever over some minor calamity. She probably tickled me as she dispensed this bromide. I still take a deep breath and repeat the magic words to myself when I know I have to weather a particularly difficult time.

Proverbs, the sayings in Benjamin Franklin's *Poor Richard's Almanac*, church hymns, and goodness knows what other sources were the basis of her endless supply of conventional wisdom. I learned in Spanish class, for example, that "the proof of the pudding is in the eating" was written by Cervantes (perhaps he got the idea from his grandmother). The year I made a raid on the closet holding all the Christmas presents, I painfully learned she was right when she told me that "curiosity killed the cat."

So much of her "wisdom" seemed to have to do with birds, cats, and dogs. For example, "If you want to get the eggs, you have to keep the chicken." I must have used this phrase a thousand times. I think Woody Allen used a version of it once, and I bet anything he got it from his grandmother. Of course, I was never "to count my chickens before they hatched" or "try to teach an old dog new tricks."

She challenged my progressive spirit by cautioning me that I probably couldn't "make a silk purse out of a sow's ear." She pulled my reins back when she wanted me to look before I leaped. She tried to teach me prudence with "a stitch in time saves nine."

I adhered to my grandmother's philosophy because it seemed she was always right. I did have my day once in a while, I did benefit when I planned ahead, I did learn that ugly words are just that, no more. And even if her prophecies didn't always turn out exactly right, she made me feel so much better.

When I was in college, one of my friends' dads decided to punch a hole in my tidy guide to living. When I would spout one of my grandmother's teachings, he always responded, "Ah phooey." This was heresy to me, but he was a charming man and I allowed what I thought was his little joke. Our bantering on the subject became so animated that I began to call him "Ah Phooey" and referred to his contrary way of looking at things as "The Wisdom of Ah Phooey." Everyone in the family started calling him by my name; and when he and his wife wrote so much as a Christmas card to me, it was affectionately signed "Mr. and Mrs. A. P."

You know, he did have a point; contrarians usually do. After all, sometimes you might want to take the chance that you can have the two birds in the bush, and if you let sleeping dogs lie, you just might miss a good show. If I were to take Ah Phooey's advice and end up with egg on my face, my grandmother would surely have found a way to make it all right with some just-right saying. More, she would make it right with love and good humor.

I often find myself dispensing advice or making observations with the blessing, "as my grandmother would say." But once in a while, I throw my head back and with blithe abandon blurt out "Ah Phooey." After all, I don't want to put all my eggs in one basket, do I?

Spreading
WINGS

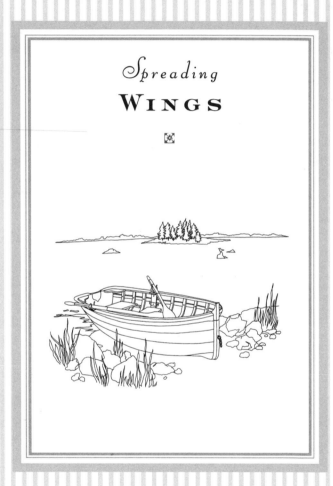

"Does that girl ever stay in one place?"
Mr. Crozier, our electrician, asked my
grandmother one day. "I see those
skinny little legs flying by my shop all
the time." I did fly free about my
neighborhood growing up. I did fly
free when I took wing and went into
the world beyond that store with its
pretty lamps and dazzling hanging
chandeliers and all the other familiar
places where I felt safe and sheltered.
Wherever I have gone I have searched
for those friendly faces like Mr.
Crozier's, who looked out for me in
their own way—who noticed that I was
about my journey with purpose and
direction. And, luckily, I have found
them.

LIGHTING A PATH

The Methodist church we attended was an uninspiring brown-stone building kitty-corner from my grammar school. A number of people we knew went to this church, and it became the heartbeat of much that we did. Once my grandmother had a little fainting spell at the top of our basement stairs. She landed in a swoon, and barely before she came to her senses—unhurt, thank heavens—the minister was walking in the door. We had called him before the doctor.

The kindly Reverend Jackson, who pretended to be far sterner than he actually was, had baptized me, and my religious education began under him. Every Sunday we were marched down to one of the first pews. My stepmother believed in sitting up straight and listening to every word of the good minister's sermons. They interested me from very little to not at all, and usually I was already a little churched out after Sunday school; but I did like Mr. Jackson very much. I thought him the kind of man born to wear vests and church robes, and to turn his young parishioners into God-fearing adults. His wife was also a believer in straight spines and sat with ramrod posture throughout the service. When we visited the parsonage, as I often did on an errand, Mrs. Jackson was always ready with lemonade and cookies, modest hospitality that suited her somewhat austere personality. By the time I was old enough to pretend to sing in the choir, Mr. Jackson was nearing retirement.

I liked the idea of wearing the crimson robe with a crisp white starched collar every Sunday and marching down the aisle of the church en route to the choir loft. The choirmaster was very lenient with the junior choir, not demanding very much musical talent. I, however, had none. Even so, I went to choir practice and took part in Sunday services, trying not to be heard. Finally, all agreed that I might be putting my time to better use in the service of the Lord.

Mr. Jackson was often puttering about the parsonage, next door to the church, when I hurried by to and from school or the library. He always waved to me, but I noticed under his battered old hat as he raked leaves or pulled weeds from his spring garden, he was getting much slower. Talk at home and in church circles was he would be leaving us soon—unthinkable to me: He had helped to raise me; no one could possibly replace him. I would hate not having Mr. Jackson in the pulpit, even though I had practically memorized every one of his sermons.

Finally, his retirement was official, and the church board began the search for the new minister. My stepmother probably had something to do with the deliberations, she was such an active church member. On a chilly Easter Sunday, Reverend Jackson, his eyes tired behind his clean, rimless glasses, his hair snow white and parted close to the middle, began the sermon we were all expecting. It was to be the last time we heard it from him. He was happy, he said, to see so many of us in attendance on this fine spring morning when white lilies made even our humble church grand, and he hoped that with a new minister we would change our ways and become more regular. He did not know who that was to be or when he would be coming, but perhaps the new man would encourage us to come more often, not waiting for a time to show off our finery. Each year, we got pretty much the same sermon at Christmastime too. God would be so pleased to see us every Sunday, he reminded us.

Even though I had a string of attendance pins, I felt a little guilty about sitting in our second-row pew with my new red spring topper on and a navy-blue hat I just loved—it was shaped like a flowerpot with a tiny bouquet of flowers on the side. At the end of the service after the collection, at least Reverend Jackson would be glad for the throng's above-average gifts; and at the benediction, the chairman of the church board came forward and asked everyone to stay seated. He asked Mrs. Jackson to join her husband in the front of the church. Then, in a voice barely able to choke back tears, he announced that the new minister will be the man now coming down the aisle with his wife and children. I turned my flowerpot-clad head along with everyone else's to see a tall, handsome man in an army captain's uniform walking toward his father. Everyone in the church cried, and we all hugged each other. If my stepmother knew of this decision, she had not told us.

And so, I continued to be reared spiritually by the Reverends Jackson. I was at the parsonage more often now, often baby-sitting the new minister's two small children. Reverend Jackson gave the prayer at our grammar-school graduation, he waved me off to college, he provided a seamless continuity in the life of the church and our lives that were so closely tied to it. One time, however, Reverend Jackson was to be at odds with my grandmother over me.

It happened because Sister Catherine came to live with us during her mission to America. Sister Catherine was an English Methodist churchwoman, and we all came to love her; for a time I wanted to be just like her.

Sister Catherine

Reverend Jackson asked my parents if it would be possible to have Sister Catherine stay with us while she worked with the church's missionary society, raising funds and awareness for her work. An eyelid did not have time to drop before this good woman was sitting at the big round kitchen table at 1055. She stayed with us for some months, and I began to sit at her feet, attracted to the selfless work she had done all over the world, especially in South America.

Thin and spare, as if being more ample would be out of keeping with her calling, Sister Catherine's appearance defined sensible. I quickly learned that, as a Methodist sister, she was not akin to a Catholic nun except in her devotion to the church and her work.

I began to want to dress as Sister Catherine did, reaching for the simple blouses and wool cardigans in my closet. No one seemed to take much notice of my attachment, even my declaration that I would study Spanish in high school. And while Sister lived with us, we were naturally drawn even closer to our church and our minister.

Reverend Jackson was now including me in the workings of the missionary society, and he and I began to talk seriously of my walking in Sister Catherine's shoes. I spent hours talking to him about it, and his passion for missionary work led him to encourage me perhaps more than he should have.

"I am going to study to be a missionary," I told my grandmother, revealing the plans the reverend and I had discussed. I told her I wanted to help people in the jungles of South America come to God and to a better way of life. She listened, and eventually she realized that I was far more serious than she had at first imagined and that our minister was probably fueling the fire of a young, perhaps misguided, ambition.

"If you are to be a missionary," she said in her matter-of-fact manner, "you are going to have to change your personality." She reminded me that I had not liked Girl Scout camp because it was too "harsh." Living out of doors did not appeal to me, that was true. She brought to my attention—now it seems funny—that I was petrified of insects and fearful of snakes. "South America is much different than you imagine," she announced, as she prepared rolls for supper. "I know you admire Sister Catherine, and you should, she is a wonderful person suited to her calling. And I know you want to please Reverend Jackson, but you must be sure your reasons are good ones." This was the talking to that made me realize I had gotten carried away with my romantic notions of a missionary's life.

My grandmother and the minister had a discussion about his and my plans, and I guess he realized she was right about knowing me better than he did. Sister Catherine stayed with us until she returned to England, and then to her work. We kept in touch with her for years, sending little presents now and then. None of us forgot the trip we took with her to Canada, when she was almost arrested.

It seems that her passport was good only for travel to the United States. We got her into Canada all right, but on our return, the authorities were very suspicious of this Methodist sister, my grandmother, my stepmother, my sister, our church friend Julie, and me. What did they think we women and girls were doing, smuggling a missionary into the country? It all got set right, but we had some tense moments for a while, wondering if seeing the sights of upstate New York and Canada had been worth this international incident. Sister Catherine insisted it had; but then, she was a veteran of South American jungles.

Sister Catherine's sojourn with us made me realize that, no matter how willing the spirit and no matter how much admiration you might have for someone, it is not that easy to walk in their footsteps. I have a deep and abiding respect for such devoted people, and that is how it should be. That is her legacy to my journey. I still went ahead with my plans to study Spanish, and I took classes in Latin American history and literature in college. Maybe Sister Catherine had something to do with it.

Julie

Having Sister Catherine in residence brought many of the churchwomen to our door, especially Julie. A widow for many years, Julie, by then retired, was one of the women who cooked at church suppers with my stepmother and grandmother. She attended almost everything at church, including our Girl Scout skits. She was there applauding when I played a dreadful girl up to no good at a bake sale. I think I was so cast because I had dark hair—a holdover from the nineteenth-century tradition of blonde and blue-eyed heroines. Julie practically became a member of our family. She stayed with us when she was recovering from surgery. I helped her brush her long black hair with just a strand or two of cranky gray.

Julie was one of those women I could not imagine as having been young, she was so perfectly middle-aged. Under ample bosoms, she had a large stomach, always corseted. She made her own clothes, and her dresses always included a belt of the same material worn high above her waist. She chose strong cotton fabrics for her frocks, sometimes stripes, sometimes shirting patterns, little prints in a white background. Julie loved white, and she painted everything in her house white, except the beautiful mahogany furniture in her living room. Her home looked so clean and fresh that my sister and I often visited her to hide out in her kitchen from my stepmother's assignments.

Because she knew our family so well, she was sensitive to the fact that both my sister and I could sometimes be overprogrammed, and she was glad to see us pop in at her door. Walking the dog was a favorite excuse we both used. Those little short Scottie legs happily trotted to Julie's to help steal some restful moments. As Julie's large hands smoothed sheets that had just come in from the line, I sat and talked to her. Julie was a good listener. It was to Julie that my sister revealed that she was in love for the first time, it was to Julie she took her young woman's heart. The rest of us found out later, but not from Julie. She kept secrets well. I don't think she ever let on how many times she had made potato pancakes for us or put into the oven cinnamon-flavored crusts, a by-product of her pie baking.

No holiday celebration would have been complete without this sweet woman. And she supported all my stepmother's projects at the church and elsewhere. Julie belonged to us, and we to her. It was to be so for a very long time.

A THIRTEENTH SUMMER

Three different people this year gave me copies of the same book—two were Christmas presents and one was for my next-door birthday—about Lake Waramaug. That speaks for how well my friends understand my love for that special place in northwest Connecticut. I grew up there—in its awkward stage and mine. It was something of a sleepy place without much cachet in those days, years before it attracted the local squires, who built sprawling summer houses right on the water or on the hills that rise like crystals surrounding the lake. Now even folks all the way from New York City have homesteaded there, and real estate prices are "over the moon."

The book, by the way, is written by an old friend, but not from my lake days. I worked with her in the city many years ago, but she came to the lake long after I spent my thirteenth summer there.

Year after year my family summered at the lake. My stepmother particularly enjoyed it there, and she made us pack up each year as if we were going on a pilgrimage to the Holy Land. Among the things that went into the old Nash was her fishing gear. We all fished at the lake, whether we liked it or not, and I didn't much. Too impatient, I think, to sit quietly; too lazy, I think, to get out of bed at dawn and sit in misty mornings shivering while waiting for a bass to bite. My stepmother must have believed that fishing helped build character.

But fishing was not the only activity, thank goodness, and until my thirteenth year I looked forward to our summers at the lake. My sister and I at one time or another had summer boyfriends. With these we banded together to hike around the lake, dig for nightcrawlers for fishing expeditions, and explore the lake in our rowboat. Of course, we swam every day in that clear, clean blue water dotted with stands of white birches along the shore as far as the eye could see. We swam even when soft drops of warm summer rain dimpled the surface, though Grandmother wouldn't hear of swimming if an electrical storm was brewing.

But it was the boat trips clear across the lake that used to intrigue me. (I am writing this before reading my friend's book about the lake because I want to remember things my way and not be influenced by her research, which I am sure is impeccable.) We often landed our rowboat on a spit of land occupied by an abandoned house, windows broken here and there, paint mostly peeled off its clapboard siding. The first time our little gang arrived in the tall grasses that surrounded the house, we felt like true explorers. Who belonged to this house? We would lie in front and spin tales about its past. It was obviously nineteenth century, and it had been a grand place then, sitting tall on its peninsula with no neighbors. This relic became my dream house. Of course we never went inside. It was locked tight, and we would not have trespassed, though we did peer in through the windows. But mostly we just lazed around, a little tired after rowing across the lake. Often we brought books and sprawled on the lawn to read, as if we had just left a lovely luncheon inside and someone would soon bring us lemonade and cookies. The house always gave us a destination, which was a very necessary thing to have during those endless days. No matter where we went, night or day, we felt safe. Our boundaries were our lake.

Like every idyll, this too was bound to end. My sister was pulled away by the attractions of work and the independence that came with her own hard-earned money. Imprinted on her like a baby duck, I followed; but the big attraction for me, even at that early age, was the fund I was building for my college education.

"I don't want to go to the lake this year," I announced at the beginning of the summer when I was thirteen. "I want to stay here with Daddy, and maybe get a summer job of some sort." Like my father, I would come up on weekends. This proposal was not well received by my stepmother and grandmother. First of all, neither was willing to entrust me to my father's care that summer. Both thought that I worked too hard in school and that I needed the summer to relax, away from my self-imposed studiousness.

"You need to get some fresh air in those lungs," my stepmother said. "And," she insisted, "you look pale. I want to see that nose out of a book, young lady."

So that summer, as in every previous summer spent at the lake, I was up before the sun fishing in the early-morning mists. I was allowed to substitute peanut-butter sandwiches for perch more often now, a sop to my need to define myself. And I was allowed to read about as much as I wanted without lectures about ruining my eyes or needing more exercise. That summer I had a very nice boyfriend, bookish like me, and we walked around the lake it seemed a thousand times. When my sister came up on weekends, she and I paid visits to our deserted house. Her boyfriend that year had extra innings in a post-lake season, but not many; the lake was one world, the rest of our year something else altogether.

My thirteenth year was my last as "a kid." The following summer I took a job with a family on Long Island Sound as companion to two small boys, with whom I lived, even on some weekends. My carefree summers at the lake are preserved between the covers of photo albums, but those precious times are vivid in my memory. I have, of course, returned often over the years, although my family stopped going there eons ago. The lake has stayed almost as nature intended it, though the water is no longer pristine. Several times my husband and I have come close to buying land and building there, always knowing that it would not be the same. My dream house is no longer; several contemporary houses sit on its spacious peninsula. But many of the rambling old inns still operate, and we occasionally spend a night or two in one. Not too long ago an office friend mentioned he had a house on Lake Waramaug, and as he proceeded to tell me about the lake and how wonderful it was, I softly informed him that I knew because I had grown up there. Seeming not to hear me, he went on, caught up in his own rapture. I didn't mind sharing its magic.

I will find out all kinds of things in Mary's book. I am going to wait to read it this summer, visiting the lake in a new way, looking back to its glory days. I'll have a few of my own chapters to add. And I'm happy that I was forced that thirteenth summer to put my face up to the sun and reach for the stars on those perfect summer nights. I wouldn't have missed it for the world. But, dear ones, I still don't like to fish.

THE KNITTING CLUB

Men and women in white coats and banded caps clustered around the dresser in my hospital room. A few days earlier, a seven-pound-and-some-ounces little boy had been born. Laid out in preparation for his trip home was the infant wardrobe I had spent months knitting: A white snug bunting; a yellow sweater with a cap inappropriately ruffled for a buster of a little boy; what the knitting book called a "sac," which had tiny white ribbons woven through the stitches—these elfin things and many others fascinated the doctors and nurses attending me. My obstetrician, normally so very professional, melted at the sight of all those stitches lovingly made.

We bundled up the little lad and home we went. Several of the things I made seemed silly even then. A long lavender coat with pearl buttons and rosettes on the bonnet had to wait for my son's cousin Barbara to be born. My husband's kind but firm stare made me realize his son was never to leave the house in such delicate attire. No matter—I enjoyed the knitting.

Coming home from the hospital tucked carefully in his mother's stitches, my son came to think of hand-knits as his birthright. I have pictures of him at five and fifteen in sweaters I always seemed to make just a little shorter than he needed. Impatient to finish the project and see how it looked, I often bound off prematurely.

I learned to knit early; I learned to love knitting later on. When I graduated from holding my hands out in front of me, yarn secured by my thumbs—but not so tight that it might stretch—my grandmother taught my sister and me to knit in earnest. We made afghan squares to near madness. They were for good causes, she assured us, and they were excellent practice. I took to the sisterhood of knitters better than my sibling. Her squares were often so tightly stitched that we could hardly get them off the needles. Mine, on the other hand, were neat rows of stockinet stitch, one row knit, the next purl. Nonetheless, we both graduated to stocking caps with ribbed borders—knit two, purl two was the lesson here. Mittens came next, when learning to count and knit on three needles advanced us to an entirely new level.

With these dear ones by my side, I loved to spend an afternoon knitting. With a piece of work growing wondrously in your hands, good sturdy yarn to work with, talk comes easily and time slides by just like the yarn coming off your needles. While some knitters crave complicated patterns of multiple stitches and colorful yarns attached to their work with dozens of bobbins, I prefer the sturdy, practical kind of knitting that lets me go along deliciously on automatic, row after row, enjoying the companionship that knitting with others has always afforded me.

During my freshman year of high school, a group of us formed the Friday-night knitting club. We were the sensible girls who had not yet found boys—or rather, they us. Knitting was our refuge. By ninth-grade standards, we were wallflowers. All the better, I now think, because those were great times. We met at each other's houses—always an occasion when my turn came, because my grandmother made one of her mile-high gooey cakes. Our skills varied, as did our personalities. Marilyn, whose mother was a fanatical knitter, turning out coats, dresses, and suits for her pretty daughter, was herself accomplished. The Metcalf sisters, from my Girl Scout troop, smiled a lot, just alike, and sat back waiting to be amused. Barbara, our most sophisticated member, led us astray as the year progressed, and soon we were phoning the boys without dates, giggling hysterically. All through that first awkward year of high school, we knitted our hearts out.

Of course, the knitting club gave way gradually to the demands of growing social lives. Thank goodness I found like souls at college. While others made friends at bridge tables and the like, the soft lounge chairs in the dorms were the preserve of knitters. I got help with my boyfriend's argyle socks; my expertise came in handy with cable-stitch sweaters and putting in a Vneck for a man's sweater—to this day a source of great pride. We rarely made anything for ourselves. The products of our efforts were sported up and down the eastern seaboard by lads who probably would have been just as happy with a purchase from J. Press.

Several years ago I was reunited with a friend from early working days in New York. She broke into a broad smile when she spotted me, grasped my arm, and confessed that she still had an unfinished piece of knitting I had talked her into decades ago. All true knitters, I told her, have a piece of knitting we promise to finish some day and would never dream of giving up on. That has its merits, too, I assured her (and myself).

When I was at college studying history and literature, I never thought that someday knitting would be part of my job. As a crafts editor for a large magazine, I created patterns and found wonderful knitters to bring creativity to my readers. The girls in the knitting club would have a laugh at my expense over that— as would my first boyfriend, who bravely suffered through wearing (at least several times in my presence) bulky socks with ill-fitting heels. I have often wondered if knitting remained a friendly part of their lives too. I wonder if any of them patched up a spat with a father-in-law by knitting him a vest sweater that was just the right weight for the chilly nights of a Florida winter. I wonder if their babies were warm and toasty in their own sweet stitches. Remembering the knitting club and all the knitters who became members of my own association of stitchers throughout the years makes me thank my lucky stars that I was a serious girl with good grades who learned her knitting lessons well. I still like to burrow in on an autumn afternoon, a fire going, tea at the ready. Knitting grants me such lovely permission to be peaceful.

The Night of a Thousand Stars

The low voice on the other end of the phone was dramatic and pleading: "My dear, can you possibly do fifty centerpieces for tables at the Rainbow Room. It's for a charity, of course, so there's really no budget—and apples are the theme of the evening." Yes, I could do it.

As a magazine editor I have been coming up with ideas at the drop of a hat to satisfy such requests. Each year I face some thousand blank pages all crying out for fresh material. While I get a great deal of help these days, there was a time when I was the spinner of magic.

How "the class brain" ended up as the impresario of school dances from junior proms to fall frolics I now have no idea. But my first extravaganza entailed glittering thousands of cardboard stars of all sizes. My unsuspecting committee enlisted the help of all their friends and for weeks before the dance we glued and glittered. Then just before the dance, an occasion I viewed as the most important in my life, we hung our galaxy at various levels from the ceiling of the gym. In the center we hung a mirrored revolving ball that reflected all those tiny specs of glitter. It was smashing, and everything I had dreamed about came true. Girls in strapless dresses and skirts of taffeta and tulle and boys in tuxedos completed this night of magic.

The decorations were such a hit I got the decorating chair of every dance after that. Once I convinced my crew to construct a little park smack in the middle of the dance floor. On sod we had talked a friendly mortician out of, we placed benches where dancers could tarry between numbers. Pots and pots of flowers snuggled down in the grass completed our oasis. For winter carnival, only the king and queen were crowned with glitter. The dance floor was majestically transformed by ice sculptures donated by the chef at a local hotel (probably for credit in the program). The regal splendor was right out of *Doctor Zhivago.*

I never enjoyed the dances as much as I loved producing them. By the time my tenure was in full swing, my high-school boyfriend was off at college, and I now could throw myself into each evening, taking care of details rather than participating.

Was it a natural progression from the mastery of the high-school gym into producing pages of fantasy for a magazine? In some ways yes, but more significantly, I think, I had been schooled for years for this role by my stepmother. From her uncanny abilities to take on a challenge, enlist willing hands, and see an event through to completion, I saw just what one could do. Fifty centerpieces with apples? A snap. With one hand tied behind my back.

My stepmother was a joiner who quickly moved from committee member to committee head to president of whatever organization she became a part of. Under her leadership wondrous things happened. She energized everyone, and always her family. The women of our church became buzzing bees producing a bazaar like no one had ever seen, or even dreamed of. A few cakes, cookies, and crocheted baby bonnets would not do for her year. Months ahead of time, churchwomen started quilting and canning. By bazaar time festively decorated booths were manned by chirping attendants with all manner of handmade wares. There was a chicken dinner the night the bazaar opened with her mom's famous apple pies and a dramatic presentation by our Girl Scout troop (naturally she was the leader). Our troop had our own booth for selling our homemade candy. Needless to say, this was the best bazaar ever, with more money raised and everyone having more fun than they'd ever had while working themselves silly.

It was, however, the tie sale that was to be her crowning achievement. I don't recall if it was her original idea or whether the concept had come from the headquarters of the Cancer Society as a fund-raising idea. What matters is that she pulled off a remarkable undertaking. My sister and I, all the girls in our troop, all the members of the ladies' society in our church, all her parent-teacher friends (she became state president of the PTA), every committee she had ever served on—all were enlisted to collect ties, sort them, and man the tables at the sales. We canvassed neighborhood after neighborhood going door-to-door for ties.

Wives got a chance to give away ugly ties their husbands liked; men gladly gave us the gift ties that hung in the back of the closet. No matter, someone else might like them. Local cleaners took out spots, and the volunteers met night after night at our house and at church to sort and pack them for the sale downtown.

Friendly persuasion for a good cause convinced the police to rope off several downtown blocks for the two-day sale. All culminated in a celebrity auction, for while we were collecting ties from dads and uncles, we were also writing to men like Frank Sinatra (a bow tie) and Arthur Godfrey (a Hawaiian tie) and getting wonderful contributions that fetched goodly sums. (I could have picked up some beauties at that sale for my tie-loving son who searches old clothing stores for just the models we had by the thousands on those tables.) Then, all I wanted to do was see the end of the sale and have our lives get back to some kind of normal before the next project began.

Learning by example, I began to understand what inspired my stepmother. Once she envisioned what she wanted to do, she was possessed by the dream. "It could be so great," she would say. "I can see it now," she would reassure us. She had an uncanny ability to sell her ideas and get all involved into having a wonderful time working toward the goal. I have seen my schoolteachers in our living room working more like pupils under her tutelage. If there ever was a woman who was part pied piper, it was the one bringing me up to have a love of the extraordinary.

And so it seems I came by my abilities "naturally." Once I achieved the glory of that night of a thousand glittering stars, there was no stopping my taste for creating magic. A five-foot magician taught me everything I know. By the way, the apple baskets were lovely; Patricia, Susan, Mary, and I almost jumped with glee when we saw glistening high above Manhattan the baskets we had spray painted silver, tied with big bows, and filled to overflowing with green apples.

Fond Farewells

There was no way to know when I met Etta Sweet that she and I would become friends and work together for four years. Etta was in charge of the bakery tearoom where, thanks to my grandfather, who had prevailed upon his friend the owner, I was given a job. The charming Hungarian bakery was actually managed by the tyrant Mrs. Jacobs, who always wore a black uniform. Despite Etta Sweet's sparkling white uniform and her name, she was not all sweetness and light. I was in awe of her ability to do all the cooking for the restaurant and at the same time keep track of the five waitresses, all women who had worked with her for years. At first, she regarded my help as a dubious addition.

Etta did not spend much time in idle chitchat and certainly did not praise me. To be truthful, she didn't seem to focus on me much at all. Although, I found, in time, I was able to charm the dreaded Mrs. Jacobs, such guile was wasted on Mrs. Sweet.

The other waitresses were all mature women. One was Austrian, with a charming accent; one, a French Canadian, with beautiful red hair and petite features; and one a large woman with a huge lacy handkerchief that bloomed out of her pocket. From the start they were my allies, helping me bus tables when I got too busy, taking difficult customers, and giving me tables they knew would leave good tips—because I needed money for college.

Helping each other out created a bond among us. We covered each other's stations, we pitched in when someone was sick: We were a team. Etta stayed at her grill, putting out our orders with record speed and almost never making a mistake. Through her square, frameless glasses, she also never missed a move we made. Once, when I was helping out behind the counter, I made the error of placing a wet hand on the ice-cream cooler while making a milk shake with the other. I got such a jolt that the shake spattered all over the counter and the customers. By the time I "came to," Etta had the situation in hand, the counter cleaned up, and the customers happy—or at least willing to forgive my youthful blunder.

That summer flew by. Working six days a week and getting ready to go to school kept me busy. I loved going to work, where we waitresses had our jokes, our secrets, and our daily travails together. Just before I was to leave, it was Etta who suggested we all go out to dinner. I was surprised and pleased, since this dinner was my send-off to college. And as far as I knew, the tearoom crew had never done such a thing before.

The restaurant Etta had chosen was elegant compared with our tidy little tearoom—white tablecloths, stemware, and windows that looked out on to the water. We all looked special wearing our best attire for this evening. At first it was a little awkward seeing everyone out of our familiar surroundings. But before long we were the friends we had become over the summer, and I was asked a thousand questions about school. Were my clothes packed? Where would I live? Would I miss my family too much? When dessert arrived, presents appeared as if by magic—a beautiful blouse, cuff links, little things that would remind me of my summer friends.

For four years, all through college, I came back to work at the bakery during vacations. Even Etta hugged and kissed me when I came and went. What I realized years later, long after I no longer returned to that gleaming little place with its black-and-white floors and chrome fixtures, was that the generosity I received came from women who knew that I was going on to something they would never be a part of, except through me. My future, my dreams, became part of theirs.

The fondness that went with the farewell of my tearoom friends has never left me. It is a reservoir of goodwill to which I return whenever I must bid farewell to the young people who pass through my life and are going on to places I cannot go except through them. Oh, I wish them such good fortune, and so, I know, do all the Ettas of my life.

Remembering Summer's Last Dances

We have a room that is an archive, a treasure trove of objects we cannot seem to part with. Once this room was a garage, but someone with an automobile too big for its slender proportions made it part of the house, and for the nearly twenty years since, we have filled it to capacity—with objects on its waiting list for occupancy. Chairs too good to be given away are stacked upon each other, and bolts of fabric stand in the corner, a reminder of the time I fell in love with a pattern and feared that someday when I wanted yards of it, it would have been discontinued.

Every now and then I venture into this annex, thinking that at last the moment has arrived to make use of our reserve possessions. Recently, I decided to open a cedar chest I hadn't looked in for years, since getting near it requires an adventurer's temperament. My husband, legendary for his car-packing ability, also has a talent for ingeniously stacking mountains of things on top of idle surfaces.

This is the chest that holds forgotten mementos, long buried at the bottom—the fabric bunny with ribbons given to me the night I was voted best student in my high-school class. As I pick it up, I ask myself why in the world I would keep such a thing; but then I tell myself it doesn't take up much room, so why should this be the day I part with it?

Farther down, I discover a cotton dress with a full skirt in a very soft shade of green. I used to starch this dress so stiffly it almost danced by itself when I wore it to the Pleasure Beach Ballroom so many years ago. For a few moments, as I hold this now-wilted fabric on my lap, I cannot but wonder if that magical dance hall is still there. I remember its giant french doors opened so we could dance with sea breezes flirting about us, an image that seems incongruous with today's music. Strains of Madonna at the Pleasure Beach Ballroom? On this muggy summer day in the middle of Iowa, miles and miles from Pleasure Beach, my recollection does not permit such revisions.

The music I recall is very much like the melodies my parents must have danced to some years before. And, of course, there were the sweet and sentimental contributions of my own generation. Because we seem to conjure up scenes in slow motion, that is just how I see my seventeen-year-old feet moving along the wooden floor, as close to the open doors as possible. Images of sea and sky and moon and cool night air are what come to mind with this simple dress in my hands. And while I don't think there were Chinese lanterns in that long-ago darkness, I make them part of my thoughts now, turning the ballroom into a brilliant memory.

I question whether any of us really know when we first learned to dance and when it was as easy as it was meant to be. I am sure I was an awkward partner, and at the time I probably wished I was home reading on the swing on our porch. Nonetheless, I danced those last dances of adolescence on a stage that was nearly perfect in a dress with a full skirt and tiny puff sleeves and a slip of a peplum, which I still have stored in this chest.

I am glad my husband keeps this vault so cumbersomely guarded. It is meant for infrequent musings, for a hot afternoon like this, when at summer's end I am comfortable with this reverie. I do not think I will take the green dress from the cedar chest after all—it really doesn't take up much space, and I cannot imagine what I would ever do without it.

DOROTHY'S DAD

All those tearful nights at camps from the time I was ten should have told me that I did not transplant well. Even now, the thought of moving still strikes fear in my heart. Because we are becoming so crowded in our work spaces, it was suggested recently that we move offices. When my face betrayed my anxiety, I was told not to worry—others would be making the move. I returned to normal. Transplanting is a trauma.

No move was more traumatic than leaving home for college. It was with complicated feelings that I packed for that journey. I had rooted so well at that big old house. My grandmother, who shared my dreams of a college education, was also my anchor. While my departure from loved ones was surely no different from all my freshman classmates', that realization didn't seem to ease the pain that started somewhere in my throat, the place where tears almost choke your breath.

As always, I did what I was supposed to do, putting one foot in front of the other, stepping off with the hope and understanding that everything was to be all right. At first, it wasn't.

Three of us scholarship winners were piled into one not very ample room. Since I arrived last, a top bunk was my only option. But it was neither the bunk nor the room that was to be my nemesis. The two young women who shared my first days away from home were the same girls I remembered from camp. While I was trying to fold my blanket correctly, they were already out on trails or winning swimming contests. Competitive with each other before I even arrived, my roommates began the inquisition that transformed my fear to terror. Had I picked up my books yet? Had I filled out this or that registration form? While I stammered, almost paralyzed, they rattled on and on about requirements they had already met. Oh my goodness, I was surely on my way to ruining my college year, if not my life, if the judgment of these two was the standard.

Every test became a grand comparison. I was not faring well up on the top bunk, trying to study at a little bed table my grandmother had packed off to me. Always a good, even a superior student, I was now facing a challenge I'd never met before. And there was no loving advice to come home to each day, just two superegos who seemed like monsters.

Some kind of good sense surfaced in my red-hot mind near meltdown, and I requested a room change. It was too crowded, and I was the odd girl out. My request was granted by some wise soul, and Dorothy and I became roommates, hers having left a belowground ample room, fleeing in reality as I was doing in my head.

We both waitressed in the dining room to help defray our expenses; so most of the time we wore white, starched uniforms. If I try to imagine Dorothy, she appears to me not as the mother of five children she became, but as a tall, slightly awkward girl, with chestnut hair and kind, dark-brown eyes in that shapeless white dress, gleamingly clean.

I liked this plainspoken girl with wry wit from the first. She was next to the youngest in a family of six. Her father was a New Jersey dairy farmer, but one with an unusual background. A graduate of Columbia University, he had been a school principal. When he married Dorothy's mother, they decided to take their love of learning and family to the quiet pastures of New Jersey's farm country. When I visited them for the first time, it was like living a scene from *State Fair.*

Mr. Steele was a self-contained man who said little. He

moved about his home and farm with purpose. His wife was a chatty woman who had been a teacher. Raising six children had kept her skills of instruction and management alive. Freezers were filled with roasts and homemade pies; shelves were stocked with canning from last summer's kitchen garden. Dorothy had helped, and her older sister, with young ones of her own, had undoubtedly scheduled a visit to lend a hand with the chores and get her only sister off to college.

When milk was poured at the table from big white ceramic pitchers, I was cautioned not to drink it. "My children grew up on unpasteurized milk," Mrs. Steele informed me, "you are not used to it, and we've bought milk for you." I felt safe and taken care of immediately.

One of Dorothy's older brothers was home from the army that weekend with a friend; they both disappeared to the pasture to help Mr. Steele. Her youngest brother was obviously the family treasure—an open-face sandwich, my grandmother would have called him. Billy was friendly and talkative, more like his mom than the more taciturn males in the family I met that weekend. He asked me a million questions, and he made his sister laugh and beam all at the same time. Here, with her adorable brother and her steady, solid family, Dorothy had none of the tentativeness she sometimes displayed at school. How difficult I think now it must have been to leave this oasis of sanity and be thrown in with silly girls wearing brown beanies and little signs around our necks in those first weeks of school. She had been reared to do the world's work with good humor. She had been taught a no-nonsense reality.

On Sunday, we all gathered in the dining room for midday dinner. Mrs. Steele was prepared for whoever showed up—army friends, college roommates, Billy's pals. Dorothy's dad served all our plates family style, carving the roast and giving us ample portions from heaping dishes of mashed potatoes and fresh vegetables. Sitting next to him, I observed how massive and gnarled his hands were. Heavy farmwork and repetitive milking, before milking machines relieved him of that task, had made hands that once simply turned the pages of books into the roots of giant oak trees.

I thought about Mr. Steele's hands and the farm when I returned to school—so much so that I wrote an in-class theme that week about how much I admired this hardworking man who had chosen to live in such an independent way. His hands were a symbol to me of his dedication to his own ideals and to his family. His hands were beautiful.

Some years ago I received a letter from Dorothy. We had kept in touch only occasionally in the years when we were rearing children and building family and careers. Her father had died only a short while before at a venerable age, having passed the farm to the son who returned from the army to work alongside his father. She wanted me to know that her mother had asked that her husband's hands not be visible during the funeral services because he had always thought them deformed and ugly. Dorothy reminded her mother of my college freshman essay and how I had always told her how much I admired her father and of my respect for what those hands represented. His hands were a powerful statement of his life. Mrs. Steele needed no more convincing than Dorothy's remembrance to allow all who knew and loved him to see him as he was.

Why did Mr. Steele make such an impression on me? Perhaps because I have always appreciated the expressiveness of hands. I'm sure I could identify anyone I know in a second from his or her hands alone. Once I was having lunch with a work colleague, an artistic gentleman, who froze me in a flourishing gesture to comment that I had the hands of a sculptor—that my hands looked strong and efficient. I was flattered but embarrassed, because I am not very dexterous. Looks can be deceiving.

Dorothy married right out of college. We were all excited when her romance began in our sophomore year, because she'd had no time for frivolous activities like dating. She had agreed to be "fixed up" for a date for a school dance. We all clustered about the receiving desk where the men checked in, to see the chosen escort. He was tall, handsome, and looked anything but frivolous. Together they raised five children and helped to bring up her sister's seven, after their mother's untimely death. Yes, Dorothy was reared to do the work of the world, and with commitment and good humor.

The Club

Some old neighborhoods hang on to their dignity in their declining years. The town houses around Dupont Circle were gracious dowagers living on borrowed time in genteel poverty when I alighted on the doorsteps of one. There were rows of houses just like the one I was to make my temporary home when I arrived in Washington for one of my first jobs. Many were owned by the club where I had signed up for room and board for $27.50 a week, and all were filled with young starting-outs like me.

Because I have always had a soft spot in my heart for old houses, I didn't mind at all the slight shabbiness of my residence. I thought of the house with the steep front step and pillared entrance as a lady too proud to give in to changing times. There were eight of us, all in single rooms in this particular house. All but one of us were in a hurry to get going in our lives and careers.

We took our meals in a central hall where we also picked up our mail and paid our bills. The building had doubtless been a mansion mimicking the grandeur of the embassies along nearby Massachusetts Avenue. Now it was a beehive of comings and goings, and lots of meetings and greetings. Like so many other members of the club, I didn't know a soul in Washington when I first arrived. It didn't take any of us very long to have chums to go to movies with or meet for dinner at special times. It was good we were all "in the same bucket" my grandmother said with her Nebraska good sense.

I couldn't help thinking, when I moved in, of the movie *Stage Door* with Katharine Hepburn and Ginger Rogers. In that film, all the occupants of a New York women's club were young actresses eking out an existence until their first break came along. Most of the women in my house had far less glamorous aspirations. One young German woman worked in some diplomatic capacity; another was a gemologist for the Smithsonian. I once went to see a case of precious and semiprecious stones she had painstakingly assembled.

We were stacked up on three floors. I started out in a wonderfully large room on the first floor next to our resident Rosalind Russell. Most of the time she wandered around in a chenille bathrobe with floppy sleeves calling one or the other of us to our only phone next to her room. Her exasperation with our lives may have reflected her disappointment in her own, for she had made living at the club a permanent installation rather than just a stepping-stone. One hates to think how many of us bright-eyed types she'd seen come and go. Before long, I asked to move to the top of the house next to the more sedate gemologist and further from the phone and the young men in the basement apartment with their loud music and parties. It hadn't occurred to me that the heat might have trouble getting up that high, but I wore heavy socks and sweaters and, in the main, enjoyed my garret dwelling.

When I went back recently to revisit the club, it was, of course, gone. The houses had been dolled up, inherited no doubt by today's more prosperous government workers. I was happy to see the kiss of fresh paint and the blooming window boxes, and a little sad that the club, which had been so good to me in those first months in a strange place, had given way to changing real-estate values. It had been so much easier to be out in the world with a lot of company. It was nice to open my wings just a bit slower with the club as a sanctuary. If I had been in an apartment by myself or with just a roommate or two, I would have missed some wonderful times and associations.

Someone always knew of the best and cheapest new restaurant where you could get real Turkish coffee. We could take turns picking up our dry cleaning; we could always find someone with whom to take in a movie. While my German housemate and I were not the closest friends, we did stay up late at night planning her wedding. She was far from home, and we were her support group. I was a bridesmaid in an awful powder-blue net dress with high spike heels I detested. I got up in them for her, and ended up catching the bridal bouquet, which lasted in my room longer than the wedding attire. When you needed a shoulder to cry on, our Roz Russell was always there, her soft side as worn as her chenille robe.

The garret room in the old dowager house appealed to my romantic side; when I wanted to, I took myself to Paris and pretended I was a writer on the brink of discovery. The beaux-arts architecture of Washington must have been my inspiration. Because my living expenses were so modest, I could afford to drive my English bread-and-butter car on weekend trips along the Blue Ridge and shop the sales in the swanky stores on Connecticut Avenue. It was in one of them a few years later that I bought my wedding dress. And there were the free things just blocks away: the gardens at Dumbarton Oaks, where I went every moment I could to wander in the formal gardens and the natural meadows; the Impressionist art at the Phillips Gallery, which became like my own living room I went there so often. I would have been very lonely without the club in that white stone city.

We all blew in and out of the club like fresh spring breezes. Soon it was to be my time, too, and three of us moved into a row house in Georgetown we rented from a woman going to live with her daughter in Europe for an extended time. We stood before the owner as she instructed us when to take the drapes down and send the slipcovers to the cleaners. With the owner, we counted every aged pot and pan and then signed the inventory list. By the time our landlady returned to recount her property inside this slim house (where the three of us felt like Gullivers in Lilliput), two of us had decided to get married and one to return home.

I'm sorry the clubs are gone. Descendants of old-fashioned boardinghouses, they gave many young women a safety net after college. This generation doesn't need them, most likely, and real-estate values in cities probably make it economically unfeasible. But I'm glad I found my way to the corner of P Street and Dupont Circle. It was a stop on my journey that brought me friends, confidence, and the chance to catch up with being grown-up. All this for only $27.50 a week.

THE KINDNESS OF STRANGERS

It did snow that Thanksgiving. And we did go to Grandmother's house. But as we made our way through the snow, it was not a dapple-gray that guided us; rather, we drove in a drafty little English sportscar along the eastern seaboard. Every so often, a gust of wind blew the snow through the canvas side curtains, dusting our clothes with powder.

Grandmother's house was no longer the old Queen Anne in which I'd grown up. After my father died, my stepmother moved to Florida, where eventually her mother joined her. But for a while, my grandmother lived in a smaller house in Connecticut—in part, I think, to stay near me and my sister. I was living in Washington, D.C., and I had invited a young navy officer to spend Thanksgiving with us. I was sure my Nebraska-raised grandmother would welcome a fellow Midwesterner stranded for the holiday.

When we arrived, like orphans in the storm, our feet nearly frozen, my grandmother settled my friend in an upstairs bedroom, tucking him under the eaves amidst rose-patterned wallpaper and piles of handsome quilts. From the first moment, her clear blue eyes gazed on him approvingly; she was not very approving of his tiny car, however.

Our Thanksgiving guest had never been to Connecticut before, and he was charmed by the coziness of the landscape. Iowa, he told me, was very different, save for the northeastern corner, where he had grown up the son of a county-seat newspaper editor. There, dairy farms nestled in rolling hills, somewhat like those in the Connecticut countryside.

There is no need to dwell on his joy in my grandmother's cooking. And though I am sure he missed his mother's table, he relished every meal, all of us lingering comfortably over cups of coffee. He and my grandmother often seemed transported as they talked about familiar places and memories. I remember thinking, if I look out the window now, I will be on a snowbound open prairie and not in a sleepy New England town.

It was surprising to me how little I knew about this quiet Iowan who was then a casual friend. But on long walks across the stone bridge and along the green and while chatting in my grandmother's parlor, I began to see how much he reminded me of her in his Midwestern wit and disarming presence.

Our return to Washington was uneventful. At Christmas he took the train to Iowa, and I returned to Connecticut, missing my cordial companion but not his silly car. My grandmother chose this occasion to give me the diamond earrings she had worn for half a century, realizing before I did that Thanksgiving had been a new beginning for me. I wore them for the first time the following July on my wedding day. They did not sparkle nearly as brightly as my grandmother's knowing eyes.

In three decades the images of my wedding day have never dimmed. I need only open our picture album to experience a flood of precious details—my grandmother in a polka-dot dress and white cotton gloves, my groom in starched naval-officer dress whites. But there is one very important person whose face never appears in the well-loved pages of my wedding album. And without her, I might not have been married on that July day.

Although I belonged to a large church in the center of Washington, I had my heart set on an intimate wedding in a small and beautiful country church. So I wandered about the countryside in my little English bread-and-butter car until I found the perfect chapel—a sanctuary on a knoll with emerald-green lawns and windows as tall and graceful as the surrounding trees. It seemed a hidden treasure, just waiting for me to discover. Of course, my desire for a pastoral wedding meant that guests would have to travel some miles outside the city, but I thoughtfully scheduled the ceremony for late afternoon, giving everyone—even my notoriously late uncle Douglas and aunt Irene—ample time to find my idyllic setting.

It would be a perfect affair. A simple lace dress, a Victorian nosegay of delicate white rosebuds, freshly picked flowers blue as the morning sky for decorating the church, and medieval harpsichord music filling the air—these were the details I planned with such pleasure.

When that July day finally dawned, I arose confident that all was orchestrated. I spent the morning visiting with family. In early afternoon, my attendants and I emerged from the hairdresser's crowned with yards of white netting to protect our freshly arranged locks from a sultry Washington day. Dressed in shorts but bearing a remarkable resemblance to beehives, we three girls then packed my tiny car with dresses and hats and shoes and flowers for our safari to the church.

As we traveled along Georgetown's crowded Wisconsin Avenue, filled with tourists and shoppers, my two-toned tan car, which I had purchased for its beautiful red upholstery, simply stopped. This temperamental vehicle had a history of nervous disorders, so my first reaction was annoyance rather than panic. But the latter quickly set in at the gas station where a frustrated but unsentimental employee announced he could do little for my car—or for us mysteriously coifed women.

Adversity, I have found, brings out character. My maid of honor—my delicate college roommate known for a reticent manner—took control, imploring the young man to drive us to the wedding. As my friend saw her chances of walking regally down the aisle in a divine ice-blue dress fading, her pleading acquired the fierceness of a lioness. The attendant was unmoved. We remained marooned.

Just as our hopes for rescue were dimming, a woman buying gas surmised our predicament. She came forward and quietly offered to take us to the church, even though its country location was considerably out of her way. She didn't say much during the trip, assuming the demeanor of a chauffeur. Perhaps she was reflecting on the shopping we had interrupted, or perhaps her own wedding day held some secrets.

Through this woman's firm navigation, we managed to reach the church nip and tuck ahead of the guests. I had to dress quickly, but I did walk down the aisle exactly on time. (Aunt Irene and Uncle Douglas missed the ceremony entirely.) My flowers looked lovely in the late-afternoon light, as ethereal as the medieval music that accompanied me down the aisle. At the front of the chapel, a young man standing strong in a uniform groomed to perfection turned and sang to me of his love and joy, filling my heart to overflowing. It has been more than thirty years now, yet in all this time I have never forgotten the kindness of that stranger who delivered us to the church, who was invited to stay but gently took her leave.

THE MOVIE MEN

"Do you remember the movie men?" I asked my grandmother one afternoon as we sat close to each other on my antique love seat. Her mouth formed a little pucker, the kind of expression one oft assumes when just a bit embarrassed, and her eyes shifted toward me and turned upward. "Of course I do," she answered. "Would do it again, too," she added, snuggling closer to me.

My grandmother and I had arrived at a stage in our relationship when we looked back more than we talked of the future. She was more settled into her hips than she used to be, and she would sit quietly now for longer periods of time, twirling her thumbs. I always told her what was going on in my life when she visited me; she smiled and nodded, but I think my hectic work schedule was more than she could honestly take in. Everything I did was "wonderful," the word she would use when I told her about a new assignment or a promotion. She would have expected no less from her girl.

And so we recollected. It reaffirmed our love for each other, the way renewing wedding vows after twenty-five years of marriage does for some folks. On this afternoon, I brought up a subject we hadn't mentioned for years.

While my sister and I were living with my grandmother, just after our parents were married, she had signed us on to be in a movie. This filmmaking was not in Hollywood, but in North Carolina. Akin to the enterprising photographer who once canvassed neighborhoods with an appealing pony, seducing mothers to get pictures of frightened children perched atop the animal, these filmmakers came to town luring mothers (or in our case a grandmother) to pay to have their darlings in a movie. After the shooting was completed, the movie ran for weeks in a local theater. Naturally, all the relatives signed up countless times to see the film.

All the children wanted to be discovered as future stars—at least, that is what their kin assumed. Our new grandmother was as avid as anyone else in her determination to see us "in the movies." Actually, everyone probably got their money's worth because the little film was pretty well scripted, the traveling movie company brought child actors to star in it, and the rest of us were extras who couldn't do too much wrong.

I remember squirming (a ritual that would continue for years) as my grandmother fitted me for new dresses she made for the movie. She brushed wisps of hair from her forehead as she feverishly worked in the summer heat at her Singer. One dress was the prettiest shade of peach with a huge bow at the back.

During the shooting, which seemed interminable then (the dressmaking squirming was nothing compared to my impatience while waiting in the hot sun as packs of kids ran over hill and dale to include as many of us as possible), my grandmother stood like a soldier guarding the princesses. Well, she had made us look like royalty, hadn't she? Each morning we were scrubbed and primped, our hair brushed into perfection. Making the movie was not nearly as much fun as going to the theater to see it.

Obviously, by some sweet deal with the theater owner, the short was played for weeks before the main feature. The three of us went time and again—and then my sister and I paid our dimes and quarters when even our grandmother lost passionate interest. Seeing ourselves on the silver screen was a joy we had never dreamed of. And by golly it has never happened again.

As we sat there giggling over the experience, my grandmother still insisting that we were prettier and more talented than the children the movie men had brought with them, I realized that this silly thing was probably the experience that brought us together. It was the script that our loving lives together were to follow.

My grandmother believed in dreams and possibilities. As soon as she came into my life, she caught me up in her indomitable optimism. She also showed me that behind the dreams is grit and determination. When there was anything in her power to do for me, she never let me down. Some things are beyond understanding, and I shall never truly know how she came to give so much and love so unselfishly. After all, she could not look into my eyes and see her mother's or her sister's, as natural grandmothers can. We did not have that. I think sometimes there was something in each of our makeups that found each other—was I by nature her perfect foil?

"How can I ever repay you," I asked her once, "for being in my life?"

"Repay me?" she shot back. "You brought such joy to my life, silly girl; there are no debts between us." She put her hand to the back of her head, to tidy the little roll of gray hair, slipping a hairpin out and repositioning it. I had never mentioned this before, knowing that it would make her uneasy. My grandmother did not abide such fancy ideas—what she did hold to was belief in the folks she loved and an undying loyalty to which she commanded all her resources, including her sewing machine, apple pies, Midwestern good sense, and, yes, her charm. Imagine this sensible woman falling for the movie men with all her heart and soul!

But how happy I am that the movie men brought us together in such a whimsical way, spinning the fiber that was to become my lifeline time and time again. Would that I could sit in the dark with her next to me now waiting for her to poke me gently as the little girl with the bobbed hair brushed to a fare-thee-well pops briefly into the frame. All arms and legs and not knowing where to look, I was not better than the lead actors, despite my grandmother's "Mama Rose" protestations. I did try, though, and in the end, measuring up to the task was all she ever asked.

And so our recollections about so many things were to be our symphony as our years together wore on. We were both getting older; my world widened as hers narrowed. What we meant to each other was the music in each of our lives.

A

QUILTED

Legacy

Being interviewed by the New York
Times *is not something that happens
every day. So I was a bit nervous when
I met the gruff reporter who asked me,
almost before I sat down, "Who did
you marry?" I thought it an odd question to put to the editor of a new magazine, but I responded politely as two of
my associates looked on—a little puzzled, too, I might add.*

*The reporter was a veteran of many
years of listening, and as I told him
about marrying into a Midwest family
with deeply planted roots, he seemed to
understand that I had entwined my
own more tender ones with my husband's. That is how he began the arti-
cle. He was a perceptive man.*

When I moved to Iowa, the bonding with my husband's family began in earnest. I was to spend blissful times in the home where he had spent happy boyhood days. I was to learn his history from his beloved aunt Mary, eldest sister of his mother, Lucile. Indomitable, she had stayed home through the blistering summers and frigid winters, too Iowa-stubborn to admit that the weather was ever a deterrent. My in-laws set out for warmer climes, giving in to their creature comforts. But, after all, Lucile was always the adventurous one, Aunt Mary would comment. I felt at home with Aunt Mary, she was so like my grandmother.

A FAMILY ROMANCE

Lucile's Grand Tour

The well-worn brown-leather volume with a huge map of Europe folded in the back fits comfortably in a woman's small hand, or in her pocketbook. The gold lettering on the cover, now faded, reads "My Trip Abroad." The ruled pages, originally blank, are filled with graceful handwriting that tells the familiar tale of a young American woman's "discovery" of Europe. Between the lines is another tale, even more timeless, of friendship, sisterly affection, and romance in first bud.

Kaye's little gift to her friend, my future mother-in-law, is one of my guides to Lucile's grand tour of 1929. The other guide is her photo album, filled with black-and-white snapshots, hand-colored postcards, and other memorabilia patiently assembled.

Everyone in the family, me included, has heard her stories countless times and everyone in the family has souvenirs of this Midwestern schoolmarm's great adventure. The book and the photo album, bequeathed to me not so long ago, have yellowed with time, but the passion that Lucile felt for a dream come true remains as fresh and vivid as this quick description of her arrival in London: "Morning of sight-seeing just finding our way to the city by the *tube* to Piccadilly Circus. Bought some gorgeous blue violets that were large & fragrant." I see that bouquet crushed to her face as she inhaled its aroma as if for the first time.

Many Americans still felt the postwar euphoria of the Jazz Age, as did this teacher of high-school French and drama who was, like the century, in her twenty-ninth year. She had left her Iowa and Nebraska charges several years earlier to teach in

California, so her sojourn began aboard a Union Pacific train that departed from Los Angeles. Before joining the tour led by her University of Iowa French professor, Doctor Bush, she stopped to see her family in Iowa, getting off the train in Boone. "My family is so sweet," she wrote, noting that her young brother Jack had grown "so tall" and that her pretty youngest sister Anne was "wispy."

For her sweet family, she shopped as if on a mission during the entire summer trip. In the back of the little book is a ledger that records several requests and what she spent on each item—seven pages in all! When I make a mental inventory of things we all have from Lucile's grand tour, I think she must have amassed a huge steamer-trunkful of mementos. But more of that later. She did not go to Europe merely to shop; she went to see such breath-taking sights as the fleet of fishing vessels off the English coast, which thrilled her from the deck of the SS *Megantic.*

It was the 1920s after all, I'm reminded, as I turn the pages filled with notes dutifully entered with the little pencil that must have accompanied the book. Her jottings tell of shipboard antics—skits and dances and hilarious costume displays—that continued on terra firma. She boasts that she and her friends showed Londoners how to jazz dance at London's Café Anglais. This summer of 1929 was to be no stuffy museum tour but a rite of passage, with room even for romance.

By the time I met my mother-in-law she had been married to a minister's son for a good many years. Her children were reared in a home with good books and better Bible. While I always sus-pected that the twinkle in her eyes for her only son was a clue to a hidden playful nature, her journal surprised me in places, delighted me in others. Lucile was a cryptoromantic. On one page, she writes of being awed by the art treasures of Venice on a tour led by a "handsome Venetian nobleman." In the next passage, she describes her glee at witnessing the wedding of "a shy little bride much bedecked in white finery" in Santa Maria della Salute. Lucile presciently observed that the crush of tourists in San Marco "seemed to mar the sanctity" of the processions of priests quietly chanting their prayers—a problem the basilica finally addressed in the mid-1990s by banning tourists during services. Her good sense informed her that the gondoliers serenading tourists on the Grand Canal were a faint echo of the glory that was Venice, "which the future will cherish," she observed, "but not surpass."

Professor Bush kept his charges moving, following the predictable path of a grand tour. The wonders of Florence kept Lucile's slender pencil flying across the pages, as though these priceless treasures would disappear if she did not record her impressions of them. Delightfully, she includes humbler scenes as well: a walk through narrow streets, women hurrying from mass, men strolling with their dogs.

Her roommate on the tour, Helen, became the particular object of her good nature and exemplary kindness. Poor Helen, stricken with flu in Florence, was tenderly nursed by Lucile, who even sacrificed sight-seeing to spend time with her friend. I can see her taking on that duty without rancor but with eyes and ears alert for the sights and sounds she had yearned for while planning her trip and saving her money.

Lucile's open Midwesternness—call it naïveté, if you prefer to—led to meetings with many people; and she recorded each encounter, often from a teacher's perspective—as, for example, her innocent dalliance with a young Spaniard whom she met in Nice, where he was studying French life in anticipation of a career as a diplomat. It seems never to have crossed her mind that the young man might have been practicing diplomacy of another sort entirely while charming a slim American woman with blue eyes the shade of cornflowers.

Arriving in a misty rain, she saw Paris for the first time "thru a thin gray veil"—"just as Paris should be," she wrote. These pages, written in late July and early August of 1929, reveal my mother-in-law's heart in ways I had never before imagined. Her years of studying French, even earning a master's degree, had prepared her for these golden days. Her free spirit, always tethered by her upbringing and her profession, took flight in the cafés and shops and theaters of the City of Light. She even had her hair bobbed at "Jean & Paul's." Imagine! Oh, she saw the Paris prescribed by Professor Bush—"Paris has 35 bridges crossing one river, the Seine," she deadpanned in guidebook style—but a livelier pen recounts a jolly time at Brasserie Lipp and dinner "with the boys" in Montmartre, where "nightlife types appear." An artist sketched her picture, and George bought her roses.

("Did your mother ever mention a man named George?" I asked my husband.

"No, I don't think so," he responded, not attaching any significance to my query. He recalls others of his mother's boyfriends, names she had coyly mentioned. She was, after all, over thirty when she married, so there had been time for a romantic past. George, I think, is sealed in this little book and in a few pictures in the photo album, with "the gang.")

In Paris, days were described as "grand," and her shopping pace picked up. She bought herself a "saucy" hat. Even Professor Bush made a startling disclosure on one of those Paris nights spent dancing in cafés and clubs—something about living life fully "without fear, and without pity." Good thing Mrs.

Professor Bush was along to temper the exuberance of the moment and the *vin ordinaire*.

Afternoon picnics with George, climbing expeditions at Fontainebleau, and suddenly it was the last day in Paris. At the New York Bar "a little secret was revealed and the answer [is] to be given in two years. What a surprise! What strange things do happen!" (George was apparently too dilatory with his two-year game plan. Before the answer could be given, a shy, scholarly young journalist had won her heart in an Iowa rose garden.)

The SS *Homeric* took Lucile and her treasures and her memories home. What excitement there must have been when all the gifts were given out to sisters, parents, brothers, and friends. Of course, there was something for thoughtful dear Kaye, who had presented her with the journal. Most of the items are small things, like the cameo, purchased in Rome, that she gave me when her first grandchild, our son, was born. The bust of Mignon that came to me, my name written on the bottom, after my father-in-law's apartment was closed, was on the long list of items marked "Venice." It would never be moved as long as either of my in-laws was able to enjoy the angelic expression and exquisite craftsmanship. Linens from Brussels and Switzerland have passed from generation to generation in our family. The tablecloth she gave me, used and used, never wears out. My husband's cousin has a cutwork sheet that his wife spreads every year beneath the Christmas tree.

Lucile's generosity spans generations. We all have a piece of her grand tour. Could she ever have imagined how her halcyon days (before the economic woes of the thirties) would live on in so many hearts and homes? Lucile's romantic notions so long ago have given me the pleasure of knowing that her heart held secrets she shared only with her journal. My father-in-law survived her, writing for us a memoir that related her steadfast devotion to him and to her family. It is lovingly told. Her well-traveled heart made the right decision that day in an Iowa rose garden. Of course it would.

By the way, my husband has her cornflower-blue eyes—the best memento of all.

A Long-Distance Courtship

Lucile had no way of knowing that when she decided to marry a newspaperman, her relationship with him would make headlines. "Great Craft Plunges in Residence" was an Associated Press story on December 22, 1930. The great craft was a mail plane of Transcontinental-Western Air; and after striking some high-tension wires in Alhambra, California, on his way to landing the plane, the pilot crashed into a residence. Before the plane burst into flame, the airmen and passengers had rushed into the house and rescued the two occupants—"both fleeing in their night clothes." Then the house burst into flames. Among the fifteen hundred pounds of mail was a small package from Boone, Iowa, meant for my mother-in-law.

Lucile and Paul had known each other a few short weeks before Lucile returned to her teaching in California and Paul resumed his work at the Boone *Republican*. It was through letters, airmail letters, that their courtship continued. It was via airmail that the ring he selected from the jeweler on Story Street began its journey. It did not make it for Christmas, as he had intended.

By early February, as the newspaper account reads, there had been a "careful assortment of the mail and unscrambling of debris," and the ring was now on the bride-elect's finger. The wrappings were almost completely burned away, but the ring was in perfect condition. "At the announcement party," the yellowed newspaper clipping continues, "the story of the ring was told."

In the spring, the groom-to-be and his best man, "Mud" Benson, drove to California in Mud's Ford for the wedding. When we celebrated the fortieth anniversary of this union on a glorious June day at the university's Memorial Union, Marshall Benson (his given name) was not with us, but a couple who had attended the wedding was, and they had taken home movies of the event.

We watched the faded, flickering film, displayed the cross-stitch sampler that Auntie Alpha Dee had made for the event, and sat in rapture as my husband sang to his parents a song fellow Iowan Meredith Willson had written about settling down in a cottage "somewhere in the state of Iowa." The vision of the bride in soft green chiffon fluttering in the breeze like a butterfly, her arms laden with pink and white roses, was on all our minds as the music carried us away. We were to celebrate a fiftieth anniversary at Aunt Mary's when their grandson serenaded them with a saxophone solo, but that was the last. Although anniversaries came and went after that, their health was too fragile for parties.

The two-week courtship, the dramatic delivery of the ring were the beginning of a lifetime together spent mostly in small Iowa towns where my father-in-law owned and operated county-seat weekly newspapers. I doubt he ever wrote a story as dramatic as the one about his own engagement. They raised and educated two children and had two grandchildren—not the stuff of newspaper headlines. When my father-in-law left his paper in the town where he had been the longest and where his children were raised, he wrote an editorial for the front page thanking the community for its support and telling them that among these good neighbors and associates his family had thrived, for which he was grateful. That man could write an editorial, just as he obviously could write passionate love letters years before.

"Our Wedding Journey" is written on a page of the white book I have. On that page are snapshots of a honeymoon taken as they traveled from California to Iowa. They are both wearing berets, and the car is an adorable convertible. Their journey was so much more than that.

My husband and I had known each other for two years before we decided to marry. At the time, his parents cautioned us to wait a little longer to get to know each other better and to be sure. Much of that time we had been only casual friends, they said; marriage was too serious a step not to be better considered. We were sure they meant well, but we were amazed that they felt they were in a position to give such advice. I think they quickly rethought their son's decision to marry when reminded of their own love affair. Two years of watching their son treat everyone he knew with kindness and respect—that was all I needed to lead me to my well-considered decision. I fell in love with their son not for any high rhetoric of romance, but for his day-to-day eloquence.

E-love

"Would you write a love letter on E-mail?" I asked my twenty-something son.

"Yes," his answer flashed back.

"Why not write a 'real' letter?" I retorted.

"Because she would get the E-mail instantly," he responded. Love is winged still, and apparently won't wait for the postman to ring even once.

How odd, I thought, that this young man whose grandfather had literally courted his grandmother by mail would so quickly dismiss the old-fashioned love letter for an electronic missive. His namesake forebear had met the woman he was to marry during an Iowa summer in the early 1930s. After one week of sitting in rose gardens and taking walks in the cool part of the day, she returned to her teaching job in California, and he, a young newspaperman, began his long-distance courtship.

And now my son would prefer to sit at his computer screen writing that his love's eyes are the color of cornflowers, soft and blue, as his grandmother's were. Or that his lady fair is a tender soul, as was his grandmother, who couldn't resist buying violets from a street vendor on her first trip abroad and who was so generous that every member of the family still has a carefully selected keepsake from that "grand tour."

Would his E-love, delivered as rapidly as the beating of his ardent heart, be addressed to the young woman who whisked by me at the train station this morning, her running shoes meant more for a jog than a stroll in the moonlight? Perhaps this programmed courtship will appeal to her sense of cool efficiency. But not to me.

There's no reason that the language used in E-mail can't be as silly and sappy and sincere as that used throughout the centuries in forms ranging from hieroglyphics on papyri to the purplest prose on a lace-edged valentine. It's possible, I grant you, that the same screen on which I write my various business letters and memoranda can also emit a sentimental glow. It just takes some getting used to.

Still, I couldn't help asking myself, wouldn't my son want to write a love letter in his own hand, with my father's fountain pen—the one my son was given on his twenty-first birthday—just as my father had? Would he not want to press a flower in the folds of his letter, as his father had once done in a letter to me? Would he not want his recipient to have the pleasure of collecting his letters, tying them with a ribbon, and placing them in a box for safekeeping? Would he not want to relish the lapse of time between the letter and the response, as an eternity to hold close?

Perhaps I can convert him, perhaps not. And maybe his way is best for now. I hope, though, that his love will get a letter in the old-fashioned way. Something tells me that when he truly falls in love, E-mail will not do, and that while times may change, hearts do not. So I make a plea for love letters and a language of intimacy too delicate for high technology.

A FAMILY HOME

The first time I visited the big house on the boulevard it was summer. I had been told that Midwestern summers were legendary for sultry temperatures and soggy humidity. It was, however, hotter than I had imagined. My very first sight of the house with its great windowed front porch and rock-solid walls filled me with awe—here was a place that withstood the test of time. This was truly a family home.

My son entered this house that had been his great-grandparents' in a baby basket. As we lunched in the breakfast room, the midday sun filtering through glistening windows, he slept peacefully beside me. It did not seem warm at all that day—thick walls and shade trees outside were effective air coolers.

It was summer the last time we returned to the grand old house. It is now too big for its residents to manage, and no one in the family is left to carry on the traditions that were born and bred here—the way Aunt Mary had.

The time came too soon when the sunporch was jammed with cardboard boxes—all neatly packed, all destined for different parts of the country where relatives would receive bequests so carefully considered. Aunt Mary had seen to that. For years she had been the curator of this family home—and never has there been a better one. Even on this day, the windows sparkle like diamonds and, flung open to catch the breeze, they remind me of calm, cool days spent on that porch chatting, drinking iced tea, and eating frosted creams made with one of the family's cherished recipes. No one in the current generation has managed to reproduce the delicate flavor of Aunt Mary's.

Time appeared to stand still here—but time has run out for all of us, and today we are packing our memories along with the mementos. My son, then a college "man," helped carry out the boxes.

What a privilege he has had. Within the same walls where his father spent happy growing-up years—untold Christmases and Fourths of July—he too has enjoyed occasions blessed by a loving family's warm embrace. One Christmas, for example, he was given a game that had been his grandmother's many years before. I think that was the same year his father received his grandfather's silver penknife.

Among my most precious memories are the hours spent talking about family things, like the cracker bowl that was brought from England and for years has been a cache for Mary's rose petals, ones from her wedding bouquet and from when her daughter was born. From time to time, we have taken the perfectly pressed linens from her drawers and recounted their stories. Some stitched by namesakes, some meant for hope chests and never used, some her great-great-grandmother's. My favorites are three doilies I borrowed over the years that are mine to treasure now. So much of the texture of my life is a rose stitched by a great-grandmother from thread too delicate to imagine. It means more than faded faces in the album.

I am glad that I have listened. I am happy for every moment in this citadel of family pride. And while sadness fills my heart, because we no longer return to this tree-shaded boulevard, I look at the motifs on my linens—birds, butterflies, flowers—and remember with pleasure calm, cool yesterdays in this special home.

The velvet-covered albums sat on the marbletop table in Aunt Mary's beloved house. We often held them in our laps for long hours, poring over faces whose identities have long since passed from living memory. Now, they seem to be peopled by characters from a novel; the images appear larger than life.

I'm familiar with many of the family names: Alpha Dee

Walton, and Lennie, Lucille (Ludie), and Philamon Bennison. I never fail to spot Hercules Walton, always referred to as Uncle Herky by Aunt Mary. I have often wondered what sort of man he was. He came from the Illinois side of the family, the side where the Waltons and the Bennisons got entwined. It all started when Aunt Mary's mother, Rosa—a Walton—visited Kewanee, Illinois, one summer and stayed with relatives. There she met and married Walter Scott Bennison. (Imagine being named after a romantic novelist!) The Bennisons remained in Illinois during the early years of their marriage (when they no doubt encountered Hercules Walton), and Aunt Mary was born. The growing family then returned to Iowa to live the remainder of their lives not far from the Walton farm where Rosa grew up.

Aunt Mary never had a lot of stories about Hercules Walton; the fascination is mine. Posing for the camera in an awkward-fitting suit and stiff, high collar, his visage defined by piercing eyes, he has a presence I find compelling. Like so many men of his time, he looks childlike in his photograph. Such a strange thing for a sensible man to be doing, he seems to be thinking. I cannot help but imagine the life of a man with such a mighty name, and I ponder whether there are Herculeses in other Midwestern families—hopefully, also men great in their devotion to family, land, and principles.

And then there is Hattie Petticord, one of my favorites among all the women. There are pictures of her and several of the Petticord boys in one of the albums. Hattie is a strong, unpretentious name. It evokes meals cooked with fresh vegetables, a garden worked over in cool mornings, a family fed with homemade bread and dressed in clean, coarse-woven clothes. Hattie Petticord was of the generation of women we've mythologized as knowing the true meaning of love and having a wise, no-nonsense way of living. I question whether she was truly the brave person of my imaginings. And was Hercules Walton the shy man of strong character that his face and name have encouraged me to believe? No matter.

Still, on special days, I get out these photo albums again. Perhaps a Thanksgiving, or simply an afternoon when it's pleasant to sit by a fire, and I can dwell in another time.

The Spell of Mighty Kinsmen

One questions the exactitude of the stories we families recount year after year. One wonders what embroidery has been stitched into these yarns. Each Christmas, for example, the spirit of Uncle Ed Walton grows larger and larger, and in my mind I see him like a great Mr. Pickwick, arriving at the Walton homestead in Redfield, Iowa, his carriage laden with Christmas cheer for all.

John Ellsworth Walton, Uncle Ed, the only son in the family, was an adventurer, not unlike his father. Uncle Ed left his more timid and traditional sisters behind and "ran off" to Chicago. And he did come upon good fortune. His good nature must have been appreciated by his staff, because in 1902, at Christmastime, they presented him with

a ruby-and-silver pitcher. I've seen it polished up for many Christmases, along with Uncle Ed's reputation for generosity and the reflected happiness of holidays in Redfield.

The Walton children always came home for Christmas. Some from Des Moines and, of course, Uncle Ed from Chicago. The train stopped in Redfield in those days, and Robert Richardson Walton met his kin at the station with a horse-drawn carriage. They say the neighbors always knew when they heard the sleigh bells that Rosa Walton and her children had arrived. I can imagine them all—white fur trimming the bonnets of the little girls clad in their best velvet coats; quilts and blankets snugged tightly around everyone on the snowy trip to the farm. Those sleigh bells are still a part of our family holidays, and the very sound of them puts me among people I know only through legends, or adults whose childhoods are like fairy tales to me.

Hampers of food—smoked turkey and fresh oysters—arrived with Uncle Ed. These were true delicacies to Iowa farmers. And there were other wondrous presents for everyone. Aunt Freda, the most phenomenal needleworker anyone had ever known, brought her gifts—beautiful pieces of handwork, so precise they seemed to have been wrought by an angel.

The Iowa prairie can be a forbidding place in late December. I envision that white Victorian farmhouse in a swirl of snow, and I can feel the biting wind. But inside, there is a family together—its wandering son returned, and with him the welcome gift of warmheartedness.

It takes so little imagination to journey again to a happy time, even one we did not really experience. Uncle Ed's stately silver pitcher bespeaks a Walton family Christmas, 1902. It seems like yesterday to me, and I wonder again at those tales. I see Uncle Ed, looking just like his photograph in the family album, standing erect in a fur-collared coat and holding a grand black hat. Surely that is what he wore as he carried his Christmas baskets—heavy with treasure—into the house in Redfield, God-blessing everyone.

The Power of Love

When a quilt was needed for photography, everyone who worked with me at the magazine immediately thought of Aunt Mary. She was called, and more often than not she reached into her cedar chests or linen closet and found one of just the right color and pattern. It would be carefully wrapped in muslin, and her hands would not be hurried as she unpinned the fabric envelope that held one of her most prized possessions. Even our photographers called her "Aunt Mary," and she loved it.

For years I had intended to do a book of photographs and essays entitled *Aunt Mary's House, The Story of an American Home.* Like many another good idea, it seemed that I had endless time to complete it. Always the day-to-day demands of job and home put this goal farther and farther away. Luckily I do have a modest record of this most remarkable home. For a decade we borrowed Aunt Mary's things—tablecloths, china cups, marbletop tables—as props for our photographs. Sometimes we even invaded the premises, and a mother and baby would be positioned on the Victorian horsehair sofa. Her tulip tree would be in full bloom and full view through the sparkling windows. We photographed an old-fashioned wedding there one year, and the models we had imported from New York also became "related" to Aunt Mary from that moment on.

Years later, when I was viewing the work of a California artist in a New York City gallery, I marveled to see Aunt Mary's hardanger curtains in one of the paintings, her needlepoint lady's chair in another. The artist had obviously clipped them from the magazine for what artists call scrap. Though I did not write the book or take documentary pictures of the house, there is a record, thank goodness, that many others have enjoyed.

At first, I had to coax Aunt Mary to share her fabulous collection of needlework. She had appointed herself the ad hoc curator of a family legacy. But as the years went by and our fondness and respect for each other grew, she would sit me down of an afternoon and begin to unfold the treasures she had guarded so carefully. I felt exultation as her mother's needlework emerged, and her grandmother's, and the work of relative after relative. We sat in the sunny breakfast room where, across from the glass-top table, a series of drawers had been built into the wall. Doilies, like the one I now have with an embroidered rose, were perfectly laundered, starched, and rolled around a cardboard tube. Layers of tissues were laid back one by one for each. And there were dozens. A set of luncheon doilies with faded blue stitches was Aunt Mary's own pride and joy. She had stitched them in the 1920s and won a state-fair prize for the excellence of her workmanship. The motif, a whimsical oriental design, seemed a little dated to me, but I was awed by the quality of her work.

"When I came home from Ward Belmont," Aunt Mary told me, referring to the women's college she had attended, "I worked in one of the department stores in the needle-arts department, teaching embroidery." It was hard for me to imagine Aunt Mary anywhere but on her boulevard, among her late-Victorian furnishings in the house where her parents once lived. But she was proud of her work days, which did not last very long.

With each piece of needlework, there was, of course, a story. I guess I could say my knowledge of the history of the Waltons and the Bennisons began with their table linens and bed quilts. The hardanger panels that graced the windows in the dining room were a legacy from Aunt Freda, Aunt Mary's Uncle Ed's wife. Across the room from the panels was a walnut cabinet that held a set of remarkable hand-painted china, a gift to Uncle Ed. Each depicted a different hunting scene to commemorate his love of the sport.

"Did you know," Aunt Mary asked in her high-pitched voice, "why she was called Freda?"

"Aunt Mary, how could I possibly?" I demurred.

"Well, Uncle Ed insisted on calling her Fred, and we women in the family would have none of that. So we all called her Freda."

I had to laugh over that bit of family decorum, which told as much about the imposing Uncle Ed as it did about his wife.

"She completed twelve panels like the ones across the room," Aunt Mary told me. "For every window in her living room—can you imagine that?"

No, Aunt Mary, I could not imagine that anymore than I could imagine the fact that you still had nearly every item given to you for your wedding some fifty years ago, all carefully wrapped, most of it never used.

Hand-knitted lace, inserts in a pair of linen pillowcases, were to come to me. And there were sheets and tablecloths with embroidered motifs and crocheted edgings. Before her mother's hands were crippled with arthritis, she too had done beautiful hand- and cutwork. I love the linens I have inherited from this family as I do the handwork of my own grandmother. Aunt Mary knew, as we spent countless hours with embroidery on our laps, that my love came close to hers.

Aunt Mary and I would have been fast friends even if we had not had this special bond. She was frank, open, and salty, and I loved her for it. When a long-lost cousin began to show interest in her, she would look at me with her mouth pulled tight and comment, "Now why do you suppose after all this time I've heard from him?" We both knew the reason, and we were both amused that, with the passage of time, a yearning for family things was spreading to a new generation. Aunt Mary in her own way made sure everyone was taken care of—or not. I cannot say that I agreed with all her reasoning, but she had maintained this collection for years and it was hers to bequeath. Do not think that because I was closest to her I was given more than a reasonable bequest.

Nothing changed at Aunt Mary's until it changed all at once and was gone. There was no redecoration. There was just fanatical maintenance of floral-covered walls and oriental carpets. Not unlike the home in which I was reared, her rooms were rich with comfortable furniture, needlepoint pillows, gleaming mahogany, and china vases. The grandfather clock greeted you at the front door, the family portraits never left their positions on the mantel. Her mother as a bride was the centerpiece of the arrangement. White organdy ruffling framed her face, shown in profile. Her hair was glorious; her soft, sweet expression, captivating. All of her four daughters have something of her demure quality in their young portraits, too—all arrayed across the mantel. On a table nearby, Grandfather Robert Richardson Walton, wearing his Grand Army of the Republic hat, had pride of place. He is a man in his seventies in this classic photograph, his hair and beard snow white, his bearing still ramrod straight.

"He was a six-footer," Aunt Mary always reminded us, "and he went into the Union Army when he was just sixteen. He was so thin, he had to drink gallons of water to make the weight."

Why, one asks oneself, do we always hear the same stories? My son has begun to remind me that I tell the same story on cue. I suppose I do, but I never minded listening to Aunt Mary in the hours and years we spent together in that family citadel.

In winter, we would retreat to her back bedroom. Uncle Ed and Aunt Freda had left her their mammoth walnut bed and dresser. The room was completely windowed, so it was especially cheerful on sunny days. Two comfy old rockers were where we settled in. Sometimes she still did a little mending; I knitted sometimes, less as the years went on. It was here that we inspected quilts when Aunt Mary took a mind to.

If embroidery was the gold of this family, its quilts were its diamonds. Four generations quilted, and their work was preserved in drawers and cedar chests. Each quilt had its history. American Midwesterners prize their quilts in ways many others have trouble understanding. They are the story of the frontier experience in the "words" women chose to use when life was hard and times uncertain.

The quilts of Jenny Walton, Aunt Mary's grandmother, are spare and primitive. Several of them are log-cabin patterns, one of the most traditional, and the fabrics are rough, as if they were homespun and hand-dyed. She used a fabric until it was used up, practicality superseding design. I favor the deep reds, faded indigos, and mellow browns. In among the solids are bits of plaid and florals that have begun to look like the garden's late-autumn blossoms. Quilts were necessities first that became art later as hands and hearts poured love and devotion into them.

By the time her granddaughters were getting married, Jenny Walton and her daughters, Rosa and Alpha, were making fine quilts of cotton satine in Rose of Sharon designs with intricate quilting patterns for the hope chests of each of the Bennison girls. A neighbor, Mrs. Royer, was brought in to accomplish the twelve-stitches-to-the-inch standard that all good quilts must have. Aunt Mary and I viewed on many occasions the dozen or more family quilts, many never used. Over the previous years, all family brides were given one; I was and, to the credit of either my good sense or bad, have used it to cover my own bed for years. It is worn now, but I hope she would forgive me. Jenny Walton's quilt is worn, but used no more. I will pass it on for another bride to deal with the dilemma of displaying or preserving it. And Aunt Mary's wedding quilt will probably never be used but, I hope, kept with tender care in honor of the women in the family who made it with such perfection. I take it out every now and then to let someone see it, as she used to do for me.

Her nephew was her accomplice in keeping the house as it was when he spent his boyhood holidays there. They both puttered about the garden and prayed over the roses. The roses were her favorites; and when one bloomed to perfection, she cut it, displayed it for a few hours, then popped it into the refrigerator to keep it safe for a future viewing.

"Why, Buddy," she'd say to my husband, "we've got to get in there and do some weeding." She stood on the back porch directing him with her cane.

"Aunt Mary, this place looks better than my own," he'd plead when her demands became too much for him. But they never really did. Those two had a simpatico rare to see, delicious to be a part of. Her beloved nephew kept her old Hoover vacuum cleaner working for years. She never would have tolerated a new one, or a new toaster for that matter. Her 1930s Toastmaster is still operating in our kitchen, her faith in the technology of that period well placed. Leaves were raked in the fall, mowing done in the summer. In all seasons, the windows had to sparkle. The pair of them were in league on this. A work friend who used to run by Aunt Mary's asked me once how she kept her windows so clean. Her secret weapon was, of course, a nephew who loved her so much no task was too great.

Saying Grace

Uncle Virgil, Aunt Mary's husband, was one of the most adored men I have ever known. Not only did adults like me gravitate to his smiling countenance and generous spirit, but the children in the family, including my son, considered him a pied piper.

We have family photographs of children climbing about him as though he were a pillar. The oldest pictures show my husband and his cousins; more recent ones, my son. On the evening of his debut in a school holiday play, my son, then age seven, entrusted his hand to this kindly gentleman, a pose captured by the camera's flash.

Uncle Virgil would not miss this theatrical occasion, he told me, even though it meant driving on a blustery night miles from home. As it happened, the night turned out to be one to remember. Our young lad, frightened by being left alone in Santa's cottage, knocked it down and made his escape across the stage—to the horror of his parents. Uncle Virgil laughed, his cheeks as rosy as the rouged Santa in the play, and he made me feel that an unfortunate incident was a treasure rather than an embarrassment. And so it has become.

Holding forth on summer afternoons from a porch rocker with a glass of lemonade in front of him, or working in the yard raking leaves on a fall afternoon in a hat as battered as his old rake, Uncle Virgil was, for me, the spirit of home and family. At no time, however, was he more in command than at the Thanksgiving table.

Aunt Mary reigned in the kitchen, and a rap on the knuckles expressed her authority if you interrupted her during a holiday dinner's preparation. Help was one thing; what she deemed interference (the specialty of children eager to sample stuffing and cookies) was quite another. But what I remember most about those holidays is that when the Thanksgiving turkey was finally placed before Uncle Virgil, this simple man, reared on an Iowa farm, was transformed. When it came time for him to say grace, he became the most graceful of orators. His words, although plain, made a family of all of us—a family that included friends who had not been with us the previous year and who were unlikely to return the next. He thanked us all for our presence and for the gifts we brought him and his family, and he drew us tightly together as our hands bound us one to another.

I don't know that it was the things he said that made his words moving; he was, after all, not normally an eloquent man. Rather, I think it was a boundless optimism, a genuine gratitude for blessings that made Virgil an unrivaled messenger of glad tidings. In his presence, we realized how fortunate we were to be together, how proud we were to be a family.

When Virgil died, a cloud hung over the family. But the following Thanksgiving, my husband, whom Uncle Virgil had pushed down snow-laden hills in a sled and driven to school dances in his shiny car, sat at the head of the table. As the moment approached to say grace, I wondered if after all those years Uncle Virgil's guidance would lead my husband to the right words. It did. For the secret to saying grace is clarity and sincerity, an appreciation of the simple joys and the days we are given. Said from the heart, even the humblest words are a benediction.

The Original Jenny Walton

The cemetery near Redfield, Iowa, is on a hill, always windy on Memorial Day when we visit to plant flowers to decorate the graves of our family. There are never too many people there anymore; and in the past few years, only my husband goes. He keeps faith with Aunt Mary, who used to call him every year to inquire when he would pick her up and what geraniums or peonies they were to take there. Like most country cemeteries, it's fairly well tended, but that was never quite good enough for Aunt Mary. She and her nephew worked away on these visits; I confess that I wandered about.

"Who are these folks?" I asked Aunt Mary one year about graves near her kin.

"Oh, those are the Petticords," she responded. "Hattie Petticord was my great-aunt, Jenny Walton's sister." I recalled her from the faded photographs in the velvet-covered albums.

"Shouldn't we bring flowers for them too?" I inquired timidly.

"Why, that's up to the Petticords, dear," she said matter-of-factly and went on weeding.

We did start bringing flowers for Hattie Petticord, roses from Aunt Mary's garden. Aunt Mary kept on tending to her kin's resting places, among them Hattie's sister Jenny's, whose grave rested next to that of her husband. Grandpa Walton's grave was already usually decorated by the time we arrived on Memorial Day, a small American flag flying from a marker because he was our hero, a veteran of the Civil War. Tall and handsome, Grandpa Walton often went to town, always sporting his Civil War hat, leaving Jenny on the farm to tend to chores.

Jenny Walton was really Mary Jane Walton, and she had come with her young husband to this part of Iowa in a prairie schooner in 1869. In her arms was a three-month-old son. They made the trip from Illinois, where they had been married. For the next seventy years, she was a farmer's wife and then a farmer's widow. Aunt Mary loved her grandmother, as I loved mine. My mother-in-law did, too, I imagine, but I never felt the same connection. Aunt Mary, especially, realized that her dear grandmother was the backbone of the family, and she spent as much time on the farm with her as she could. It was Jenny Walton who taught her to stitch and cook and keep house.

If I had had the daughter I dreamed of, she would have been privileged to bear this good lady's name. How Mary Jane became Jenny is easy enough to imagine; how Mary Lillian, Aunt Mary's given name, became Mary Jane, was told to me with great love.

"I wanted to have my grandmother's name," she told me on one of our visits on her porch. "So I just decided to take it, and no one seemed to mind." Everyone I knew who didn't call her Aunt Mary called her Mary Jane.

"My grandmother made me practice my embroidery, just as she had," Aunt Mary told me while handing me a piece of white fabric as big as a bedsheet. "Look," she said as her hand traced the patterns, "every one of these is done in the thinnest white thread. My grandmother worked these in the evenings on the farm." Dozens of patterns covered the sheet, all exercises in embroidery. The motifs of flowers and birds are ones we have all seen, rendered, as they usually are, in red. These were her grandmother's impeccable white-work practice stitches.

Aunt Mary wanted her grandmother's name, and she wanted to please her with her own accomplishments. She had; her own work was incomparable. In many other ways, Aunt Mary followed in her grandmother's footsteps. She was the oldest in her family and she held everyone together. She cared for her own parents with love and devotion. She was always there for her brothers and sisters and their families. She was always there for me and mine. And while she has told me many lovely stories of her mother, we always came back to the legend of Jenny Walton's goodness and her special influence on her life. I wouldn't know these things about Jenny Walton if I hadn't learned them from Aunt Mary. She made her love part of my life, and Jenny Walton has become part of many other lives through my writing.

We don't have a good picture of Jenny Walton, as we do of Robert. She probably never took the notion to go into town and sit for a photographer as he did. But despite his somewhat dandyish instincts, his love for his wife has come down to us in many ways. Once Aunt Mary told me he went into town with a load of corn and came back with a walnut dresser for an anniversary present. She lived a decade after him on their farm, until she was ninety—years during which she quilted and canned, made frosted creams and sticky buns for her grandchildren, and kept house as long as she could. When she died, children, grandchildren, and great-grandchildren gathered in Redfield and buried her on that windy hill on a July day when the peonies and geraniums were in flower. We put Aunt Mary to rest there a few years ago next to her husband and her kin and the grandmother she loved so much she wanted to live with her name. I know she lived with her heart.

Aunt Mary was ninety-three, the last of her kind, the last of those who will return to Redfield. Going on as a family will be so very difficult without her. And at no time of the year will it seem so lonely as during the holidays.

A Brick for Aunt Mary

In recent years, the old Memorial Union at Iowa State University has had new additions, and the students now gather around food courts with pizza and french fries instead of in a cafeteria with food more like Mom made at home, though not nearly as good. And the "old botany," one of the oldest buildings on the campus—a nineteenth-century relic that had begun to look very bedraggled as new science buildings were springing up all around it—was being remodeled. Some feared the old thing would be torn down and another touchstone of the campus that was would be lost. But the old botany building now has a new life and a new face to honor one of the university's illustrious women graduates, Cary Chapman Catt. She was the valedictorian of her class in the 1890s, when few women attended this agricultural college. But she was a woman who fought for her beliefs that women should have the right to vote. Now women will study politics in these halls with fresh paint and good lighting, and they will walk across a courtyard paved with the names of women honored by individual families and groups as being "the bricks" of their time.

It is a nice idea, and I suppose it goes back a long way. For a modest sum, my husband had his aunt Mary's name carved on one of the bricks. We debated which of the women in the family we wanted to memorialize this way. Cost aside, we decided Aunt Mary, who had spent her life in Iowa, would be our choice. It meant more to us to single her out this way. And so students for years to come will walk across Aunt Mary's brick. We were asked to write a dedication and explain why we thought she belonged in this honor court. Of course, I am sure the committee never turned anyone down, but we enjoyed the exercise. It gave us a reason to remember her again.

Aunt Mary would have just given us a wave of her hand and a turn of her head if she knew why we wanted her to have a brick. What we said and what we feel is that she was a woman who believed in home and family above all. She was a wonderful wife and mother, a loving aunt, a good neighbor, and a devoted churchgoer—sixty years in the same congregation. She had been the perfect daughter and granddaughter. She kept her home for all of us to come home to. She preserved the family things and made sure we all had a piece of our heritage. Aunt Mary was a woman of her generation who knew that home and family are at the heart of life, and she kept on as she was taught. She was our bridge to the stories and gracious traditions that made us a family, a building brick that connected one generation to another. Aunt Mary's strength entitled her to a place on the court; but the love she inspired placed her there, just as it should have.

Last Christmas, a small white scroll with a red ribbon was on the top of our tree on Christmas morning. When I untied it, the nicely printed document read that a brick had been placed on the honor court at the college where I had not too many years before given a commencement address in the name of Jenny Walton. My husband was giving this gift for his two Jennies, his great-grandmother and her writing namesake, whose address that day inspired this book. So Jenny Walton has found her way from a prairie farm to the hills of Pennsylvania. Her brick belongs there, where women are building lives to face new frontiers as she once did in her own way, as we all do in our own ways.

$\mathcal{D}ear$
FRIENDS

There are volumes to speak of the friends who have chosen me. For is that not what our friends do? Is it not that choosing that makes friendship the divine gift that it is? And there is no pantheon among these chums who make our journeys with us. I have heard friends described as pillars on a porch, always needed, but also silently standing by, supporting our lives with understanding. Oh, my dear friends, how often I have felt unworthy of you all. But thank goodness you looked beyond my bluster and foibles to make my journey so much more beautiful. What a pure thing friendship is.

BLOSSOMING

The Reading Baby

Elm trees still shaded the 1920s Tudor-style house along Parker Avenue when we moved into the first home we ever owned. Coming to upstate New York from southern Connecticut, we had bid too much for this comfortable house, as sturdy as the elms had once been. The local bank saved us, and we purchased the house for a very reasonable sum. From the beginning, the three of us felt good about living there.

Across the back fence were rows of triple-decker houses; in many cases, one extended family occupied all three flats. Beyond them a Carmelite Convent stood silently except when marking the time of the nuns' devotionals with their beautiful bells. At home with my little son, I began finding the rhythm to my own day by their dependable knell. When I took my wee one out for carriage rides or walks, we met only two of the sisters, who were gardeners about the property. They descended on us with such warmth, always chatting away, I wondered about the vows of silence of this order. Perhaps when outside the walls they were allowed to be part of the community. I simply enjoyed their delight in my little lad and never interrupted our daily meetings with questions.

My ritual of strolling by the convent each day began when our son was about eighteen months old. It was then I took notice, as we went block by block, that sometimes for hours at a time, he would read off the numbers on the mailboxes. I don't think I thought this particularly exceptional since we spent the typical child-parent time with him and his little library of books and records.

As he neared two, I hired a charming young student of early childhood education to spend several afternoons a week with us so that I could work on freelance writing assignments and take care of some personal business appointments. During my mother's time out, she happily played games with our child, exercises she was learning in her teacher's training.

Nothing remarkable disturbed our little household until one day my helper calmly announced that the baby was reading. How could she possibly make such an absurd statement?

"He just read the grocery ads in the newspaper to me," she responded.

"Well, of course he can do that," I retorted, unimpressed. "When he and I go to the store, I point out all the products we are going to buy to keep him busy and interested until our shopping is done. He recognizes the shapes of the bottles and cans— that's not reading," I informed her.

She was way ahead of me. "But I have written this list of words on a sheet of paper and he had read them all off to me— that is reading," she now insisted. The list began with *daddy* and contained words like *catsup* and *sausage.* The baby was in fact reading.

In the months that followed, I watched him read everything, including the newspaper. Resting in my arms on a city bus, he read all the signs above the seats, causing a woman standing next to me to turn pale. Bedtime stories involved our selecting the books; he read to himself. Since I had never raised any other children, I thought this was special, but I don't recall being overly impressed. The rest of the world, however, kept reminding me of the uniqueness of the reading baby.

It was the children over the back fence whose recognition finally got our attention. I had an opportunity to teach part-time at a girl's high school and needed to find child care beyond the capacity of my mother's helper. When I discussed the need with our neighbor, she said that all her children were now in school and she could use the extra money to help buy her oldest son, probably then about twelve, a piano. I lifted my youngster over the back fence as if I were giving him to a member of my own family.

I'm not sure Connie and I would ever have become the friends we became if it hadn't been for this bargain. We were women whose paths probably would not have crossed except through our children. Women are so fortunate this way—to have a universe of friendship extended to them because the love of offspring unites them. Connie was impressed with the jobs I had had and the assignments I was getting. I was awed by the way she ran her home. From the back steps upward, she had the same discipline as the nuns across the street. Her Italian mother lived directly above her; her older sister, on the third floor of the well-cared-for very tall house. Our little son was in the midst of a loving family, and undoubtedly eating better than he did at our table. The youngest of the quartet, he was like the last stair step in the family. It was the two older girls, ages five and eight, that gave me my awakening.

Enterprise strikes early in children. Normally it is a lemonade stand in the summer or an old-toy or comic-book sale staged on the back steps. My adorable back-fence neighbors came up with this plan. Their friends had stood in wonder as our son read their books. How to capitalize on this phenomenon? During playtime, they pulled him around the block in their wagon, inviting the neighborhood children to bring any reading material: If the baby read it, they collected pennies and nickels.

The baby loved it. All this attention. The girls loved it because they did not have to share their profits. The main attraction was too young to understand anything but the smiles and cheers. The parents involved, however, were not amused. As soon as we all found out about it, the business was closed down. I realized for the first time that this gift was to be a mixed blessing.

By the time we moved, there was a piano across the back fence and our child was more rosy-cheeked than ever. We had all become a family, sharing holidays with both Italian and American specialties. We had a grandmother with old-country wisdom, which she imparted in exotic but crystal-clear ways— always with eyes rolled back and a hand in the air. The girls were once again innocent playmates, delighting in having a cuddly little "brother." The bargain Connie and I had made had worked out just fine.

It was Connie who sent me to the kindly monsignor who was in charge of a school for gifted children. He told us what we had all come to know ourselves, that this wee boy, now just three, was way ahead of himself in so many ways, but he was still just a reading baby—we were never to forget that. It's not easy to be different, even when the difference seems marvelous. Lots of love and understanding is what all children need; ours was to have his special reasons for a fair share.

Keeping the Home Fires Burning

That is my husband in the old photo, the timid little lad with the Sunday-school haircut. His newspaper-editor father bends benignly over wife and children. The picture was taken for

Christmas in 1942 by a small-town photographer who probably bartered his services for newspaper advertising. These bartered photographs are a priceless record of my husband's growing up. The annual Christmas photo was inserted in a Hallmark card. "Season's Greetings," it read, just as if no war were on, as if everything was normal on Main Street in Strawberry Point, Iowa.

My father-in-law rode a bike from his home to the *Press Journal* office; wartime made gasoline scarce. But that was a small inconvenience. I've always suspected that this very frugal man approved of such conservation measures. It was the disruption of life in more dramatic ways that made that Christmas an uneasy one. Boys from places like Iowa Falls and Strawberry Point were training for combat all over the country and being shipped overseas. My husband's uncle Jack, the one his mother always called "Buddy," was a naval officer and would serve in the South Pacific. Her son was the "spitting image" of him, she always insisted. Years later, when my husband was commissioned as an ensign in the navy and both her Buddies were set side by side on the mantel, we all had to admit she was right.

I treasure this photograph of Christmas 1942 so much because it is a portrait of steadfastness in a time of so much turmoil. Life would go on for those left at home, because everything *depended* on their going on. These parents would rear their children much as they had been reared, or at least they believed it was their duty to try. They were responsible for keeping the home fires burning for our generation, and they accepted that charge as if they too were soldiers defending hearth and home.

When my husband and I were parents of a young son, we faced our own time of challenge and uncertainty. We had just moved to Buffalo, where my husband was to attend graduate school. Buffalo had been a great city in the early days of the century; when we arrived, the dying elm trees along what had been gracious avenues of elegant homes seemed a metaphor for the city's decaying industries. As Christmas neared, the weather turned grayer and grayer, and snow squalls roared off Lake Erie nearly every day, chilling our spirits, as did the demonstrations against the war in Vietnam that turned the university campus upside down. Many days my husband struggled to get to the campus across town only to be turned back by police lines. Off and on through the winter, students occupied the administration building, halting the rhythmic pace of academic life.

As had our parents before us, we tried to go on making life as normal for our youngster as possible. And we delighted in the wonderful friends we were making and in the generosity and kindness of our neighbors. Buffalo may have been down on its luck in many ways, but the hearts of its people made it a place full of riches.

That first year in Buffalo, my husband and I were both so preoccupied that Christmas preparations were put off until Christmas Eve. We hauled the biggest tree we could find up the once-grand staircase that led to our apartment, two floors above a doctor's office. The red-brick Federal-style house was desperately trying to hold on to its dignity, but we were thrilled with the floor-to-ceiling windows in our living room and the working gas fireplaces. The doctor below, near retirement, came infrequently, so the house truly seemed like ours, especially that Christmas Eve.

We put the tree in the middle of the three large living-room windows and covered it with all the lights it could hold. As my husband assembled the toys, I tied crimson bows on the tree and set a little table for a midnight supper in front of one of the other windows. We lit the candles on the table just as the bells of the beautiful old church on the corner began to ring, summoning worshipers to services. As if on cue, snow began to fall, as gently as I had ever seen it fall in Buffalo that winter, and the people below, lightly dusted, looked up at us and began to wave. We waved to a steady stream of churchgoers until the street grew silent and their footprints were whited out. This is the picture that I wish I had in our album to show our son. I would place it beside the one of his father's family in that December during World War II. Each Christmas, no matter where I am, I find myself back at that window for a moment or two, rejoicing in the blessings of the season and the goodwill that bound us all together on that night so long ago.

The Year of the Fire Horse

Sag Harbor is a wistful place in the fall. The summer residents have gone, and the beach is virtually abandoned except for the hardy souls who run close to the waves or take dogs on early-morning walks. It's the ideal time for a photography shoot, a time to capture the misty autumn mornings with the romantic power of the lens.

The sun sets early, and by the time the shooting ended, the crew gathered in a cozy local restaurant for dinner. We were laughing and talking and fretting over the fickleness of the next day's weather. (The photographer and I would be up before daybreak to assess our chances of good pictures.) Suddenly, I heard my name called from across the room.

A friend insists that I am unique in the number of chance meetings I have with old acquaintances. I tell her that I have been to a great many places and know a good many people, which, I rationalize, multiplies the odds of out-of-the-ordinary meetings. But I was stunned to see Sarah, the woman who had taught me to soften lamplight with a piece of secondhand lace.

As we hugged, each said the other hadn't changed a bit. That wasn't quite true, of course. She was pale and quite thin, but her exaggerated energy was indeed the same. It had been at least ten years since I had seen her last. Her marriage over, she had taken her two darling daughters, both born in the same year as my son—one in the same month, only a day earlier—and gone to live in Paris. In her divorce settlement, she had gotten possession of this small establishment, which her eccentric former husband had won in a card game. I'd never known people like this before I met Sarah and her family.

Though we had not kept in touch, I had once seen her pictured in a French magazine in a chic dwelling. And I was aware that she had succeeded spectacularly with a book she had written. I rushed to buy the book and turned eagerly to the back jacket flap to see her picture. The young mother's youthful straight hair and long bangs had been replaced by a curly top; other than that, she had the same flamboyant air about her. But she did not look the same as we sat talking in the restaurant, separated from the rest of my crew.

Sarah's background fascinated me. A French student, she had stayed on in Paris to work in films. There she met the dashing Californian, heir to a small lumber fortune that both proceeded to burn like matchsticks. When the money was temporarily gone (there always seemed to be some ancient departing relative leaving more from time to time), they sought sanctuary back home with her family in upstate New York. That is where I met Sarah and the girls.

She wore dark tights and schoolgirl navy-blue shoes and tied her impeccably cut hair back with a scarf. Her style intrigued me, probably because it was French. Sarah tolerated a little shabbiness in her apartment that I soon came to appreciate as charming.

Loose-fitting slipcovers were made from faded old fabric; inexpensive little tables and screens were scattered about. A friendly chaos made you feel comfortably at home. And every meeting became an occasion, with candlelight and embroidered linens from a thrift shop. I suspect Sarah was the first bohemian I ever knew—she was a seducer who swept you along with her discreet charms. Her two darling daughters were part of her theater, and she dressed them in dark colors with small prints and plunked fetching hats on their blonde heads.

Sarah bewitched me with her style. She coaxed me in one way or another to be just a little less conventional. And knowing her subtly changed me forever in little ways that are hard to describe. I wanted to add just a dash of what she had to my own life, and feel comfortable about it. I think I did.

We decided that night in Sag Harbor to have dinner together the following evening. She had bought a house in the town with her book royalties, and the girls were miraculously home from boarding school. I was to see them. She also told me that she was recovering from surgery for breast cancer and was trying to work on another book. Now I knew the reason I had felt her ribs when I hugged her and why that formerly shiny black hair was dull and thin.

If my friend is right and these encounters happen to me more than to other people, I am happy for my good fortune. I would not have wanted to miss the courage and love I found in that spare saltbox house on Long Island that night. There was a bareness that was different from the old cheery apartment I remembered, but it was appropriate to the style of the house. I recall thinking that nothing seemed too permanent, but it was pleasant. The girls, then in their midteens, were as pretty as I remembered them. They talked easily with me, even though they only dimly remembered who I was.

And they cooked dinner—everything was baked, from the chicken to the baked apples for dessert. We ate in front of the fire on a bare wood table, and I could hardly keep from crying as I saw the mature way they were taking care of their mother. As the evening wore on, the younger of the two politely excused herself to study. She was the one who had nearly scared me to death when I gave her a bath on one of her sleep-overs at our house by letting out the most bloodcurdling scream. (Her sister offhandedly remarked, "Didn't Mommy tell you A. is afraid of water?" No, Mommy had not, and it is lucky that I didn't drop her into that ancient old tub of ours or that my husband did not suffer a fracture or a heart attack getting up the stairs to see what had happened.) I went out into that exceptionally dark autumn night thinking that Sarah had done a superb job raising her girls.

Sarah did get well; the girls had assured me she would. She calls me now about once a year—sometimes from Paris, sometimes from some unexpected place where she is house-sitting while she writes a book. The girls, born in 1966, are young women now with lives of their own. Sarah always reminds me that our children were all born in the year of the fire horse, supposedly the charmed year of the twentieth century. "They are fire horses," she says, and I'm never sure exactly what it means for them. But it is something good.

I'll take her at her word, because she has always tugged me along farther than I thought I could go.

Grandma Chapman

Our "triplets"—my son and Sarah's girls—were bundled up to their noses when we took them on sledding parties. All three hugged tight to each other as one dad or the other pulled them about, their voices ringing out like Christmas bells. Soon they were walking in each other's footsteps in the snow and trying to trudge in ours, their faces cheery red. We missed Sarah and the children when they went to Paris, but we had the good fortune to inherit Grandma Chapman from them.

The transition was seamless, since our little one had so often been in the company of Grandma Chapman's former charges. Mrs. Chapman was a widow who had brought a certain order into Sarah's madcap life. Barely five feet tall, she reminded me of a nanny in an English children's book. Her gray hair was tidily tucked behind her ears; and her attire was prim, even a little threadbare, but neat as a pin. Grandma Chapman's starched bib aprons, which she made herself, reminded me of my own grandmother's.

Sarah had dubbed her Grandma, so we called her that, too. I suppose I knew her first name once, but I don't remember it now; yet I can recall completely how she moved about both of our houses keeping the children at her heels. She folded their clothes in tidy piles so that they could put them away themselves and she straightened their rooms with their willing help.

Was this quiet, dependable woman a kind of Mary Poppins? I think so—her demeanor always held an air of mystery.

Grandma Chapman was hardly an employee. I would never dream of reminding her to dust above her eye level. She simply didn't do it, and it was all right with me to take on the assignment. (In her own spare but immaculate apartment everything seemed to be at her eye level.) She unquestioningly understood Sarah's ofttimes unconventional life; she came to our home with the same openheartedness. Although she never said so, I think our son was less of a challenge and our lifestyle more compatible with her own values. We came to depend on her, not just for the loving way she cared for our child, but also for the sensitive way she related to us.

Mrs. Chapman was our ballast in some days of stormy seas and change. When she ascended the massive stairway in our old house, I breathed a little easier. The gray coat she wore in winter, with her scarf folded precisely inside, momentarily made her seem to me, almost always waiting at the top of the stairs to greet her, just a little bigger than she was. The effect, when she removed the coat, was of a kernel stepping out of its shell. My husband and I looked forward to Grandma Chapman's arrival even more than our son did. She made us feel safer, happier.

But she and our boy were indeed chums. She held out his snowsuit jacket, coaxing his arms in, and helped him wriggle into his boots so they could go to the park together. Both were ready at a minute's notice on a summer afternoon for an impromptu hot-dog roast.

Once when I came home from work earlier than usual, I saw the two of them in the kitchen. Neither realized I was there. The scene was of a very small woman at the stove, her glasses perched on the end of her nose, listening intently as a three-year-old read the instructions from a box of whatever it was she was preparing. When my husband and I were invited out on a weekend night, or if we had friends over, she packed our youngster's toothbrush and pajamas and took him to her house—"So you two can sleep later in the morning," she said. From her own children's youth, and saved for her grandchildren, were toys our son had never seen before. He still searches in antiques stores, at rummage sales and flea markets for a toy taxi that she had—it was always a lure (as if he really needed one) to visit Grandma Chapman.

How sad we were to leave this good and kind woman when my husband's job took us westward. We spent our last night with her, and we all cried for miles when we said good-bye. I thank Sarah for finding her and bringing her into our lives; not having known her is unimaginable.

WOMEN'S WORK

The best meal I can remember?
At my mother's table, when I was nine years old.

—MATT LAUER
THE TODAY SHOW

By nature, I am not a collector. I do like certain things, but after acquiring one or two examples, it occurs to me that I have neither the room nor the inclination to go on gathering, so I satisfy my yearnings by admiring the collectibles of others. One little collection has, however, grown up in my life. It began with a gift from a friend and almost every addition has come from loved ones.

While visiting a dear friend in Boston, she presented me with a tiny hand-painted porcelain brooch. I was wearing a high-collared shirt and she thought I looked too severe—even for Boston. I didn't own a brooch at the time, having never had much of a taste for jewelry of any kind. But I was taken with that pin, rimmed in faded gold and decorated with petite red roses. I liked it so much, I began wearing it all the time. And to my amazement, this small object attracted considerable notice. Somehow my brooch made me more approachable, and even strangers often asked about it. Soon, in a small, sweet way, that pretty pin changed my life.

Perhaps it was inevitable, or perhaps it was simply the enchantment of my legacy, but I began receiving others—each one, it seemed, more beautiful and more special than the last. In the beginning, all my gifts were hand-painted porcelains with rose motifs, certainly the most popular design used by china painters. One was twice the size of my original; another, so delicately painted that the roses bore just a blush of pink. Before I knew it, my brooch garden had grown to include forget-me-nots, violets, pansies, and flowers fresh from the imagination of the artist. The instigator of my collection took a special interest in finding new ones; her prize catch was an intricately painted pair of lovers.

Of course, I wore them all, and I delighted in making that special choice each day. When for some reason I was pinless, it was apparently noticed and my brooch missed. I missed it, too, because that was the day an endearing communication failed to happen. Oh, how often I have heard the words, "I love your pin." And just hearing the word *love* feels good.

Many of my painted brooches were doubtless vintage early twentieth century. One, however, was made of tin and had a 1930s air about it. After that gift, newer brooches began appearing in my life. Blue stones, deep purple stones, white stones in settings with the artistry of the 1930s and 1940s are now part of this ever-growing and changing entourage.

Packing these small treasures away never appealed to me. And when one Christmas a velvet Victorian heart arrived at my Iowa home from a friend in Red Hook, New York, I believed I must have willed it. From that moment on, my pins have rested pinned to my heart. When my heart is filled to overflowing, I choose a pin to continue its journey, giving it to someone I know will cherish it. With each pin goes a special heritage and my good wishes.

Cuisine de Tendresse

When we visit a fine restaurant in France—a nation of food lovers and renowned chefs—it is the haute cuisine we seek. But one day not long ago, in a small village in Burgundy, I learned of another charming type of French cooking, called *cuisine de tendresse*.

Some days are just meant to be rare. We may not realize it when dawn breaks, but sometime in the glittering afternoon we are sure that things have never happened exactly this way before.

The morning we left Paris for a luncheon in Burgundy some two hours south, it was raining that sort of gray rain that turns the streets into a symphony of halftones. On nearly every street corner, flower sellers offered sprigs and bouquets of lily of the valley. Later, along country roads, we saw children who waved and smiled and held out more *muguet des bois*. By the time we reached our destination, the car trunk held a pretty little garden of grasses and lilies of the valley to give our hosts.

I had expected that lunch in a country house in France on such a day would resemble a light picnic. Oh, not so, my French coworker assured me. "You will," she said, "receive a traditional Burgundian meal."

I did not understand what she meant, but after a surfeit of riches in Paris restaurants and bistros I was pleased at the prospect of eating once again in a home. And I was anxious to get to know the people who had so generously invited us journalists to lunch when we had merely asked to poke around their house and garden in pursuit of a story.

Before lunch we walked in the garden. I do not speak French, but with a friend translating and with eyes and hearts and armfuls of mutual respect, we exchanged much more than pleasantries with our hosts.

We talked about beauty, what it really is, and how carefully we must guard it. The beauty of the garden was our perimeter, but I had the feeling that our congenial hosts were people with a much wider perspective. They understood matters of the soul.

Shedding our boots and rain gear, we entered a kitchen already filled with the aroma of wonderful regional dishes. There was no pomp and circumstance to our lunch. There were no skilled waiters serving on white linen. Our host placed a bottle of local wine on the table, its collar dusty from the cellar. The large square table was set simply with country pottery, and the red-and-white-check curtained window opened right off the garden, so our view was of flowers and green, green grass. Our hostess, who in preparing the meal had moved as quietly as her cat, summoned us to the table with smiling eyes and an open heart.

When I suggested that in America we would call the fare we were being served "home cooking," our host responded: *"Ah, cuisine de tendresse."* Having never heard the phrase, I was curious as to what an exact translation would be. No, no, I was told, no words in English were quite right. I should not try to translate the phrase but understand it. For *cuisine de tendresse*, at least in the context of that old stone-walled house, clearly meant kindness, generosity of spirit, and respect for the traditions of one's family and country.

I don't believe you could find *cuisine de tendresse* addressed in the pages of a French cookbook, although the recipe for *boeuf bourguignon* will be there. But the ingredients—the succulent carrots fresh from that garden in Burgundy—won't be the same. And the worn wood of the table will be missing. And there will be no scent of lily of the valley. Yet I do think that wherever there is caring, wherever there is tradition, wherever people welcome strangers to their table as if they were family, there will be *cuisine de tendresse.*

Coleen's Wedding

When Coleen, the eldest of seven children, five of them girls, was to be the first bride in a close and loving family, all her colleagues—male and female, married and single—felt a glow kindle inside us. After work hours, when we gathered to hear her plans, hopes, and dreams for an old-fashioned "back country" Irish wedding, none of her office friends needed even a gentle push to get involved; our hearts tugged us in. What followed was a wedding day none of us would ever forget.

Coleen's family, we were told, originally came from the "back country." To this day, I have no idea what that means, but a magazine editor's imagination was immediately challenged. Coleen wanted her wedding to be a joyous and not very formal affair. Because we all lived in Iowa, we translated Irish back country to American prairie in our own way. Hadn't we all been to dozens of occasions when everyone brought something? In my neighborhood, Fourth of July picnics sprung up like mushrooms after a rain, with more apple pies, fried chicken, and corn on the cob than could be eaten. Games? Somebody set up a badminton net on a lawn; someone else had coloring things for little children; musicians arrived on the flatbed of a truck from the local lumberyard. This all-American spirit was about to make Irish eyes smile on Coleen's wedding day.

Five sisters and a mother-to-be matron of honor awaited their wedding finery. Coleen's mother made each of her girls a tea-stained full skirt bordered in a wide ruffle. I, who have always loved to knit, took on the assignment of making short-sleeved French chenille-yarn sweaters for each in delicate pastels. A flowing dress with knitted sleeves was designed to offset the mother-to-be's form. Ribbon sashes would encircle each wispy bridesmaid's waist. Since I made my son's layette, I have never knitted so happily as when watching those sweaters accumulate one by one. And I knitted everywhere, including in the car, especially on long trips. When my husband and I went to parents' weekend at our son's boarding school nine hundred miles from home, he respectfully asked me to put down my dles, fearing, he said, that the little particles of yarn swirling about us would give us "lilac lung disease." In plenty of time for the wedding, my sweater output—lilac, peach, pink, palest of pale blue, and a hint of lemon—was proudly delivered to Coleen's sisters.

Suzy, one of our former associates, had moved to New York; and she, who often arranged the flowers and table settings for our magazine's photographs, wanted to create all the bridal bouquets as well as the table flowers. She brought a vast array of flowers with her on the plane. Her cake table remains, in my mind, one of her finest achievements, with flowers edged ever so slightly in gold to match the ribbons and bouquet she made for Coleen—gilt-edged white roses to go with the bride's full-sleeved lace bodice and gold sandals. Even the bridesmaids' bouquets were individual, with a palette to match the sweaters I had knitted.

Ann, by far the best baker in our circle, volunteered to make the wedding cake, all hearts. She is a tiny lass herself, and when I saw her carrying the cake into the reception on her mother's best silver tray, my own heart stopped and my prayers started that she would make it without a spill—a bit of Irish luck there, I think. Suzy tucked some of her flowers into the cake's luscious chocolate icing.

Oh, and the tables—they were to have no ordinary coverings. We all took our most precious embroidered cloths from our linen closets and set them atop heirloom quilts—each table different, each a friend's private loving gesture. And not one cloth suffered any spills that mattered.

Laura, Debbie, Gary, Ciba, my husband, and I were the caterers, and our friend Doug served as wine steward. Here, our confidence needed constant bolstering. Debbie's Irish soda and Laura's incredible hearty breads were sliced and set up in beautiful baskets lined with linen napkins. Ciba was my husband's sous-chef as he put gratins, delicately laced with ham and cheese, in the oven one after another. Flank steaks, marinated to perfect tenderness, were grilled and then sliced in bite sizes. I bought inexpensive crocks rimmed in blue and filled each one with herbed butters and cheese spreads. Gary prepared the crudités, and he and I set the buffet tables at the reception, barely making it to the church on time. A huge bread bowl full of hot spiced apples was one last touch that made this Midwestern enterprise seem more like an Irish wedding.

The marriage ceremony proceeded without a ripple—not even when the flower girl came down the aisle on crutches festooned with Suzy's flowers. Vows were exchanged, a bouquet tossed, tears of love and joy shed. At the reception, all of the "staff," who might well have been hand in hand at the time, beamed as Coleen cut her cake while my son played his saxophone and everyone sang "When Irish Eyes Are Smiling." We felt very fortunate to have a friend who let us give the things we had to give. And as friends, we all had a marriage that day, too.

THE ERROR OF MY WAYS

The older I get the more I relish sending and receiving Christmas cards. Christmas is the one time of year I seek the company of friends I see infrequently. Without our cheerful exchanges, I would lose the stories of children born, new homes made, and the dozens of other events related through merry bits of paper.

But I have not always been a faithful practitioner of the tradition begun 150 years ago in England by Henry Cole. I had a lapse during my busy years of a new career, a growing child, and countless other responsibilities. I did, however, keep hearing from friends wiser than I, and I enjoyed every word. But as the years drifted by like so many Iowa snows, I sent fewer and fewer cards, sometimes buying them only to see them go unsent. After all, Santa duty on Christmas Eve was typical of the season at our house, where we were always assembling some confounding toy into the wee hours.

College friends, former neighbors, colleagues from first jobs, these are the people we hold vividly in our memories but with whom we tend to let communication slide. At least I did, until one Christmas, when a wonderful woman put her foot down. Betty wrote that she would be sending no more Christmas cards to my house until she heard from me.

No more Christmas cards from this friend who once knew all the secrets of my young heart. No more accounts of family goings-on from her Maryland home, of the children's achievements, her husband's career, the dream house they were building next to the ocean. No more reminiscences of our good times together or of the comings and goings of friends heard from during the year. It was enough to make me realize how clever Henry Cole was to have invented a Christmas card with his good wishes, even if he was too busy to include his usual personal messages. The year Betty issued her ultimatum I began in earnest to send cards again. I was too smart to lose a connection with a person who has the purest smile I have ever seen.

For a good many years now, I have looked forward to the December afternoons when I write my cards—and, yes, sometimes they are sent very close to Christmas Day, and, yes, they even go out between the holidays. On a table in front of the fireplace, the pile of white envelopes stand, like a fresh snowfall awaiting footprints. Soon each will have a name and address and a little handwritten note tucked carefully inside. I have been very blessed, and there is no better time to remember that fact than at the holidays.

I wish I had the eloquence of Robert Frost, who wrote to friends in his own magnificent idiom, instead of relying on store-bought greetings like the rest of us. One year, in a Christmas letter entitled "Christmas Trees," he told them he had had an offer from a city dweller to sell his wood, "the young fir balsams." Of course, he could never let his slopes be bare of his beloved trees, so he refused. But to his friends he said:

> *Too bad I couldn't lay one in a letter.*
> *I can't help wishing I could send you one*
> *In wishing you herewith a Merry Christmas.*

Once again, it is Christmastime and lives are being exchanged. And once again, I have Betty to thank—for her understanding that all my heart needed was a firm nudge when a busy life seemed all important.

Caution

Despite the efforts of family and friends, I'm not sure I ever learned to be as prudent as I should be. When I was in graduate school, I wrote a paper about the American socialist Norman Thomas, a man my father had greatly admired. What he said about himself, I believe applies to me somewhat.

When asked why he ran for president so many times with no chance of winning, and why he championed causes that only others would eventually see come to fruition, this former minister remarked that he had a spirit of righteous indignation that would not end. I have tried every way I know how to effectively curb my passion without surrendering my ideals. Once a work colleague counseled me to give up on something we both knew was right but not popular. "Why do you go on?" she almost shouted at me.

"Because I am on the side of the angels," I impudently responded.

Well, there have been times in my life when only the angels were clapping. I have done a better job, however, curbing my indignation than my caution.

This is not the contradiction it appears. My indignation is in the field of ideas and beliefs. My caution is everywhere else, and I come by it honestly. My grandmother, along with everything else, taught me to be cautious. When we went on a vacation together and stayed in a New York hotel, we spent the first half hour checking all the fire exits and stairways. This is a wise move, and I still think about it when I check into a hotel, although I never do it anymore. She made me flannel slips to wear in the winter so I wouldn't catch cold. She feared for me when I learned to ride a bike and drive a car. She worried when I went out on a date with some young man who would be driving me somewhere and could be careless. One year, on New Year's Eve, I was involved in a minor automobile accident. I knew better than to tell her about it when I got home because I knew it would upset her enough to ruin her sleep. She did wait up for me to hear all the details of the party we were on our way to when the accident happened on a slippery road. I fabricated a story about what food was served and what all the other girls were wearing, and I got her off to bed. When I told her the truth the next morning, she insisted she knew all along something had happened and didn't sleep a wink.

I am probably the only person in America who requires to be checked out in a car I rent. I hear my grandmother's voice somewhere inside of me asking if I know where the lights and windshield-wiper switches are. I never take a chance I don't have to. I read labels on soup cans to make sure the contents are still good. I am the first person to spot an untied shoelace, even on a stranger. I assume little disasters await unless I take every possible precaution. My son recently teased me before we sat down to a chicken dinner: "Well, Mom, at least we know this is going to be overcooked, and the good news is we won't get sick." I drive everyone nuts with suspicions about spoiled food; and I'm just as vigilant at the office about file drawers left open.

How can we say too much caution is a dangerous thing? I guess we can't if it is accompanied by common sense. How can we say it's wrong to be on the side of the angels? I guess we can't unless we make ourselves a pain in the neck. I'm working on both these things and hope someday to get them in just the right balance. It's a life's work, believe me.

Prudence

This is a story of a best friendship and how it is expressed in a piece of lace with an admonition. In gentler times, such reminders of virtue were often stitched in lace, in linens, and in other forms of needlework.

I have a friend who is the most forthright person with me I have ever had in my life. I have often felt that, when she exposes the consequences of my foibles, she knows I would always be much harder on myself that she ever would—and we both move on from there. Because she and I share a reverence for old laces and pieces of needlework, on one occasion she used a bit of lace to say something important.

Certainly, an occasional imprudent response is something which has been bothersome to me. Why I sometimes blunder into a situation before carefully considering consequences, I have attributed to a million reasons, including having had an idealistic father. But blunder I often do. Still, I am not totally convinced that being imprudent doesn't have its place.

Because this aspect of my character has led to some dicey moments over the years, my friend was prompted to give me a square of lace she came upon—and PRUDENCE it says. Presented after an especially awkward situation, I recall, we both laughed at its appropriateness. I still smile whenever my glance falls on it because it bespeaks our relationship so well, and I hear that kind voice trying to keep me out of a jam, one more time.

Prudence, faith, charity, hope—and dozens of other virtues were articulated in everyday items in the nineteenth century. One wonders if being surrounded by such sentiments made a difference in how people treated each other, how children behaved, or how business was conducted. It certainly didn't hurt. And the hands that stitched these letters into our lives, were they scribes of a special sort? I think of a quilt pieced with many phrases—among them, "Kind words never die"—and how that bedcover must have echoed the philosophy of a household.

My PRUDENCE square was once part of a tablecloth, and each square preached a different lesson. I hope each of the other messages has gone on to affect lives as much as mine has, and I trust each fell into hands as deft as my friend's. Are they carrying a little of the wisdom of another time into today's world? I smile to think of the word *prudence* flashing across a computer screen, and the situations that might inspire it also tickle my imagination.

In the main, we do not live in a prudent time. Perhaps yesterday wasn't either, but there has to be something to the fact that such a virtue was worthy of people's aspirations. Being reminded of good qualities surely has not gone out of style, but there must also have been something to the way it was done— with a whisper.

My lesson in lace is treasured because it is about caring. Long ago someone cared enough to design a message that just might benefit everyone by contributing a few more considerate people to the world. A few years ago, a best friend in an amusing, touching gesture found a way to use this word from another time in exactly the correct way. And I use my PRUDENCE often on a serving tray, beneath a vase of flowers, and in the many everyday ways for which it was intended. And who knows how far-reaching its instruction may be? There are times when I wish I had been given the entire tablecloth and its squares had not gone in a dozen different directions. Then, I could take on the task of improving my character in all sorts of ways. But wait, I hear my sage friend now, just how *prudent* would that really be?

Gentle
LESSONS

✖

*My grandmother did not have the priv-
ilege of seeing my son grow to man-
hood. She was really too old and he too
young for them to know each other in
the ways I yearned for in their times
together. But it was she, most especially, who gave me the wisdom to know
that I would learn from this feisty boy
with a quick mind and expressive eyes
who early on seemed to see the world so
clearly.*

*As a parent, I thought it would be my
role to help this lad pack for his journey, not thinking that he would have
his gentle lessons for me. But then,
had not my grandmother and I shared
a love that enriched us both? That is
the final legacy she left me. Neither of
us had been on a one-way trip when
we had gone "up the street" together. I*

regret that she did not get to revel in my son's wit, or that her eyes did not fill with tears when his tenderness came like a sea breeze after a rain. I miss that she did not see how much his good sense kept his mother "in line," just the way she always had. I can hear her say, "You've got a good one, there, and don't you forget it. But don't expect to get too many pats on the back, Chicken. He'll love you in his own way." And he has.

TAKING HEART

As our son's nursery school days drew to a close, I dreaded enrolling him in school. Where and how would he fit in? Surely in an ordinary class he would be out of place as children struggled to learn to read and do simple arithmetic. Our pediatrician told us about an experimental class at one of the public schools where children were brought along at their own speed from kindergarten through sixth grade. "These children are not all as gifted as yours," he said, "but the teacher is an understanding woman, and she and her assistant manage the group as if they were in a one-room school on the Iowa prairie fifty years ago. The children help each other learn." Was not this the kind of school my grandmother had attended in Nebraska? Had it not helped to make her the incredible woman she was? We rushed to enroll our son.

Five years later, parents sat in every chair in our house, and some sat on the floor, as we corralled children as best we could while the meeting continued. Our kitchen counters were strewn with enough food to keep us going through the long evening's discussion. This scene was repeated many times in the weeks that followed. The program in which our son had been thriving was being cut; budget was the explanation. We parents were not so sure that the uniqueness of the class was not the real reason. Administrators like to have everything in neat packages. Our alternative class was not exactly that.

We got to know our fellow protesters better than we ever would have without our fight. We still know many of them, and from time to time we bump into each other and check up on the progress of our children. Allan is a Stanford graduate, with a

Ph.D. in physics like his dad; Erin is a concert musician. The fear that pupils in the alternative class would not be achievers has proven entirely false. After five or six years in an unstructured setting under the guidance of two teachers, these pupils went on to junior and senior high school and compiled exemplary records. Several, including our own son, won National Merit Scholarships.

When it came time for my son to leave the nursery school in the Baptist church, he was enrolled in the alternative class. There were no traditional programs for the "gifted." A boy who had been reading since he was two was certainly that in some manner or other. One opportunity was open to us in this particular school system—an ungraded class from grades one through six. The teacher was a distinguished faculty member who had been an outstanding teacher of science and math. She had one assistant, much less experienced but warm and approachable. Our son, instead of walking to the elementary school just two blocks from where we lived, had to be bused to the school across town. The inconvenience was worth it, from our point of view.

Karen was a born teacher; a grandmother, she had a way with children that charmed the beholder. Her charges loved her and learned by her example to respect each other. Not all of these children were "gifted." Some were there because their parents were advocates of this less structured way of learning; some had had problems in other classes; and some had peculiar circumstances, like the boy newly arrived from Spain whose English-language skills needed special attention.

"Do you have a boy in your class who needs help with his English?" I asked my son one morning, learning that there was such a child in his multigrade school. Puzzled, he looked at me and replied, "No, we have Antonio; he speaks Spanish."

Antonio was not to be viewed as a child who was different; he had his own accomplishments. In that very brief exchange, I was aware of two things: First, the class had a marvelous teacher; second, my son had learned his lesson well.

All of us parents felt that our children were thriving. On the other hand, the principal of the school, among others, saw the program as a threat to good order. One group of children was doing things differently from the others. Without his support, we should have known we were in for trouble.

Each fall, the children looked forward to the astronomy sleepover. Karen got them all out on the roof of the school in their sleeping bags so they could study the night sky. This, the bike trips, and dozens of other activities kept these children actively interested in school.

On my son's first bike trip, just after he learned to ride, he spent most of his time in the van that followed along to pick up tired stragglers. Even though he was worried about his ability to keep up, he went along, Karen encouraging him. She seemed to have a special insight into our son, and staying with her for five years may have been the best thing that happened to him in his education. She knew when to let him learn on his own—a fact that drove the principal of the school to distraction when he found the child reading in the media center of the school. He would have felt fulfilled if the lad were sitting in a more formal classroom; Karen knew better.

One particular incident told us just how perceptive a teacher Karen was.

"Dad," she said on the phone one late afternoon in a call to my husband's office, "come to school with your son a little early in the morning and bring a sponge and a can of cleanser."

Dutifully the two arrived and were ushered by Karen into the girls' restroom where they both worked to scrub little-boy graffiti off the wall, written the day before in an act of derring-do. Believe me, her method proved extremely effective.

The announcement that the alternative class would be canceled came in the middle of our son's fifth year. After organizing at our homes, we began attending school-board meetings to underscore the importance of this program to our children. We all made speeches, and we were turned down time after time. Finally, we took our plea to the state board of education. It was my husband with his calm reason who pleaded our case. I kept still because I knew he would be our most effective advocate (and that I might lose my cool).

The starch in my backbone during this fight came from my own conviction and from the example my stepmother had set for me when she fought years before for repairs for my high school. I went to school-board meetings with her, standing by her side when she stood up to authority, even when it scared me. Sometimes you have to fight city hall for what you believe in.

We didn't win our battle. The alternative class was disbanded that June. In the fall, our son went grudgingly to the neighborhood elementary school for the sixth grade where his very good teacher did a fine job with him, but it was not the same. It was like a family disbanding when the alternative class was no more. We all felt a little lost.

We eventually won the war, however, because the following year school committees sprang up all over the city to address the needs of students who did not fit quite so neatly into the average classroom. Enrichment programs were created, and we felt that what we had done had at least awakened the community. Karen finished her career as she had begun it, as a science teacher in the high school, and her assistant opened her own day-care operation for a time. Our little lives went on, quite happily for the most part.

"And this too shall pass," my grandmother used to say, with a pat on my head, whenever I got my knickers in a twist over some policy that, undoubtedly, made life easier for the general run of humanity but didn't allow for unique circumstances. I have more or less made my peace with that aspect of life. I have butted my head against brick walls and connived to get over and around them; and I have also, picking my fights, just let them be. But I will always go to the mat for my kid. I learned it by example.

A Place Fair and Lovely

The two childhood friends are men now. Though both have grown tall and independent, one is strong and analytical, the other more tightly strung and romantic. But in that first spring they shared in London so long ago, they were boys of six and seven dashing across Hampstead Heath, their 1970s-style hair streaming in the breeze. Ever since, the words *fair* and *lovely* have always had special meaning to me—fostered by these two American boys' innocent views of England.

Our friends, and neighbors, had packed up to live in London for a few years, and with great joy we accepted their invitation to visit them on King Henry's Road, on the outskirts of the city. Our son was pleased to be out of school for a while, and after all, a trip to England was surely an education in itself. The six-year-old lad of our host family, however, was rather unhappy, being obliged to attend school each day in a huge, somewhat forbidding, nineteenth-century red-brick building. And while all of us adults tried to plan as many activities as possible for both boys, we heard the same plaintive cry from the young fellow each weekday, spoken with a discernible London intonation mixed with his born-in-Michigan, raised-thus-far-in-upstate-New York accent. "It's not fair [faer]," he enunciated, with his lips pouty and his eyes tearful. To this day, I can still hear him say these words and feel the depths of his despair.

School in England was difficult for him. The children mocked him for such things as eating a banana "like a monkey" and saying "sidewalk" instead of "pavement." And at recess, the other children were noisy and rambunctious, which I noticed when I went along with his mother several times as a "helping mum." The shy, slight boy found it all quite bewildering. Though for all intents and purposes he spoke the same language as his schoolmates, he was aware of the huge cultural chasm between them.

How often I have thought since then that this boy's first encounter with fairness was taking place in a country renowned for its system of justice and sense of right and wrong. Hearing "it's not fair" somehow seems more significant in a land where the rights of the common man have been recognized for centuries.

Ever since that visit, some twenty years ago, our family has had a special appreciation of the words *fair* and *unfair*. They are our shorthand for taking another look, doing it better—a tack we often take when something is indeed out of kilter. And today, the now married friend, who appeared to sense the history all around him when he was a mere boy, truly understands—perhaps more than most of us—what these intangibles mean.

And what of my son, the privileged one who was not haunted by the specter of a dungeonlike school but rather was able to immerse himself in a host of new experiences—standing with his friend across the international date line at Greenwich (shown in photographs we cherish still), traveling at marvelous speeds on a hovercraft up the Thames, gobbling scones and cream and jam in tearooms in the shadow of Windsor Castle? What was his English spring?

It was only when we were about to leave the country, packing our bags somewhat unwillingly, that we realized how he had seen England. From his first enchanted day at the Tower of London (when we were still almost dizzy from our trip over), he had a wonderful visit. And perhaps sensing that its happy times were turning into memories faster then he would like, he astonished us all with his firm declaration that he did not want to leave such a lovely place. Indeed, our own reluctance to go was worsened by the knowledge that we probably wouldn't see our friends again for a long time, which, as it turned out, was not until the boys were in college and we gathered for Christmas tea.

But "lovely"? I had never heard him use that word before. Then all of a sudden it dawned on me that during his stay he had heard that word fall from English lips everywhere. The scones were lovely, and so was he in his delight. The day was lovely and the flowers on the heath, too. Everything in England was lovely; everyone told him so. Their words made such a strong impression on him that to this day he searches in his writer's way for the "lovely" in a place and in a day. Perhaps that's why I understand how he finds it "unfair" when there is no loveliness to be found.

Prizing what is fair, pursuing loveliness in the smallest pleasures, and wanting to be with people who view the world thus—

these are the lessons the two boys learned and brought home to us in such a poignant way. Fortunately, they are qualities that linger in both men still and for which I will always thank a fair and lovely place, particularly in the glorious beauty of spring.

"Reba, This Is It!"

My friend Janet has wonderful family stories, mostly about her lovable father, who had his share of foibles. Mostly he was a big, independent personality, and he operated from his own sense of priorities rather than other people's.

Most of Janet's tales are hilarious, at least to those of us who knew her dad. They are always recited with suppressed laughter, and they always reveal deep caring on both sides. Janet's dad was usually engaged in some generous act when he got himself into trouble. For example, there was the time her brother had just moved into his "new" house, a cranky Victorian with lots of charm making up for the not-so-wonderful wiring and plumbing. Dad arrived at Christmastime with a super idea. So that wires did not have to travel all around the living room for the tree lights, he would simply drill a little hole in the corner of the room and all the wiring could fall into the basement. All agreed to the concept. No one paid much attention as Dad descended into the dark and ancient basement with his drill and ever-present stogie. As the family sat gathered in the living room, probably with their eggnogs and fruitcake, the drilling began—making a hole smack in the middle of the floor. When her bewildered and then excited brother rushed to the basement and informed his father of the "disaster," he did not ruffle the older man's feathers; Ray was ready to drill another hole somewhere else. Between the two of them, the mission was finally accomplished.

There are dozens of "Ray" stories, and I hope Janet writes them all down someday. Stories, as my good friend and truly wise woman Madeleine L'Engle says, are what bind families together. The following story is simple, but it's one that we love in our family.

When our son was about eight, our family vacation took us to Williamsburg, Virginia, and to Monticello, Thomas Jefferson's home. The day we arrived at Monticello must have been very like the one on which Jefferson decided, standing in that majestic place, that he would build his home there. The lawns were green velvet and the afternoon sky was whipped with white clouds. The tourists all about us were very quiet, acknowledging by their demeanor that this place is indeed a shrine, a monument to the genius whose achievements outstrip our abilities to comprehend them.

All of a sudden, like a stroke of lightning, a man appeared in the center of the lawn, his hands raised to the heavens, and shouted, "Reba, this is it!" He was like someone hawking hot dogs in a cathedral. He continued, by now catching everyone's attention, and presumably Reba's, "Not Sea World, not Busch Gardens, not Madame Tussaud's Wax Museum. . . ." He proceeded to recite a litany of all the tourist spots he had visited on what, until now, had been a forced vacation, and not a particularly enjoyable one. Could Thomas Jefferson have been given a finer compliment than what issued forth unbidden from this beleaguered husband? Everyone laughed, and we continued on our tour, leaving as the sun began to kiss the mountaintops.

That evening we had chosen to dine at one of Williamsburg's fine old inns. In shirt and tie, and with his hair combed as neatly as he could manage, our son proceeded to order a whole fish. The waiter, groomed as a colonial, powdered wig and all, was astonished (most children, he informed us, don't order fish at all, let alone a whole one); but he fulfilled the young man's request. When the order was ready, the waiter skillfully boned the fish and presented it to his young patron. He waited a minute or two for the first bite, probably to see if the lad really relished fish. At this point, the boy's eyes brightened as he announced, "Reba, this is it!," followed by a killer smile. The waiter was confused, but we weren't. We had one of the best laughs ever.

"Reba" is still saved in our family for what is superlative. We are careful that it always has that incredible moment of surprise. "Reba" to us is the goddess of good judgment, and to the Reba who managed to get her husband as far as Monticello that day we are indebted forever.

Tolstoy famously began *Anna Karenina* by remarking that happy families are all alike while every unhappy family is unhappy in its own way. Family stories are all alike in explaining to us who we are; but whether they are amusing, witty, or sad is the signature of each family. In any case, it is the perfect understanding they engender on retelling that makes them so valuable; it is the pride of authorship that makes them so indispensable.

Anna's Wedding

Although it is late December, it is a sun-blessed day, Anna's wedding day. Although I have been part of countless "office" weddings, none has touched my heart in a very long time in quite the same way as this one. I think it is because Anna has done all the planning herself, just as I did. Anna too lost her mother when she was very young.

We were part of Anna's wedding from the beginning. When her dress arrived, we gathered to watch her unfold the yards of satin. Her invitations were created after hours on our office computer—they were original and charming. Janet helped her tie the ribbons on each. Wedding arrangements—dozens of details—Anna marshaled like a general.

By time the petits fours arrived for our bridal toast in the office, she had everything in apple-pie order, including her work for weeks to come. We raised our champagne glasses as Anna made sure that the temporary worker who was taking her place while she was on her honeymoon was well briefed. This was perfect planning. On this balmy December day, I thought she had achieved the perfection she had worked so diligently toward.

In a way, her office family has "stood in" for her mom, by her side to share both her jitters and joys. Of all the brides I have toasted, advised, laughed, and cried with over the years, this December bride, doll-size with huge almond eyes, reminds me of what a privilege it is to be part of another's happiness. I looked forward to seeing her come down the aisle in that princess satin with flowers in her hand and the power of remembered love guiding her heart.

It was difficult to imagine that the perfect day could by its imperfection become even more perfect. But that is exactly what happened at the little church festooned with red bows and green garlands, the symbols of a Christmas Day just barely past.

We were among the first to arrive, along with the groom's parents and the photographer, so we gathered in the back of the church, none of the early arrivals wanting to be the first to sit in the pews Nicole had just decorated with a sprig of greens, a red rose, and a satin bow. Until recently, Nicole had been one of us on the nine-to-five team. Now, empowered by her months with us, she was running her own floral business, practicing many of the ideas she has seen played out in the magazine. We met her on the path as we approached the church; she hurrying off to work her magic on the tables at the reception. Later I was to learn that her studied expression masked a desperation born of a three-hour delay in getting to her assignments because of traffic jams. As I stood in the back of the church, my only thoughts of her were admiration for her work and pride that the magazine had launched her on this new career.

When my husband and son arrived, having driven there in another car, I kissed them both, even though I had seen them only hours before—the occasion seemed to invite it. I noticed how handsome my son looked, how much a man in a pin-striped double-breasted suit. His bearing took me by surprise, since I usually see him in far less formal attire. After greetings all around, our party settled on a middle pew on the bride's side. The men appeared bewildered as we three women jockeyed for positions on the aisle—places from which we could best glimpse Anna's anticipated processional. After so many months of preparation under our noses, nothing could keep us from a premier viewing of the bride.

The church filled with aunts and uncles, grandmothers, cousins, friends—even former work friends we were delighted to see. And we strained to observe every hug and kiss of recognition. The time had finally come, but the church remained very still, except for the murmur of guests on the brink of a momentous occasion. I glanced at my program and noted that the music called for was only a processional; I concluded there was to be no prelude. But the clock kept ticking, we were now well beyond the polite grace period nervous brides and grooms are traditionally given.

Green velvet filled my eyes in the next few seconds. As I looked up, the matron of honor was leaning over us. The bride would like to see my son. Would he follow her? Heads turned all around as the young man in the double-breasted suit tripped off after the vision in green velvet. My mind began to spin. It must have something to do with the music we were not hearing, but none of us really spoke to confirm this. Shortly, my son was following the minister down the side aisle and entering a little door that obviously led behind the altar.

"Oh, Danny Boy" now came sweetly from the organ—the first song I ever heard my now musician son play on the saxophone. He was obviously playing the pipe organ—but how? I wondered in complete amazement. He had taken his last piano lesson at ten, just before he discovered his horn. Carols next filled the church, and then "Here Comes the Bride" as Anna in satin drifted past us in a second.

The minister offered his blessing to the young couple, reminding them that in twenty-five years he had never officiated at a wedding when the organist failed to show up. Life was like that; marriage would be like that sometimes, too. But, he added, a friend offered what talent he had. That friend played the recessional, piping Anna down the aisle with all his heart. My husband turned to me with tears in his eyes and said he had never been prouder of our son, and neither have I. One of our office mates said she was proud of the parents of the gallant "organist." And with the sin of pride hanging over me, I am, too. He dug deep inside, called on his natural ability, and did something very hard for him—to be less than perfect. No parent can ask more than to raise a child to adulthood whose giving, even imperfectly, is done so graciously. His reward: a hug as big as Montana from the bride .

THANKSGIVING IN AMES

Winter comes to Iowa dramatically. The fall, my favorite season there, is long and teases one into thinking that crisp days and frosty, misty mornings will last forever. It is so enjoyable, you are happy to accept the deceit. When I first came to Iowa to live, my father-in-law extolled the glories of an Iowa spring. My relationship with him was always a little contrarian, so it is natural that I would love to savor autumn.

Ames is a college town, and it comes alive in September. Thousands of students change the pace of summer—band concerts, picnics in the park, neighbors chatting easily from tidy green lawns. The crimson and gold of their Iowa State sweatshirts blend with the oak and maple leaves that canopy the campus and the residential streets. All the elms died several decades ago, and by now their hardy replacements are tall and strong—in their glory in the fall. So the town has a vitality, the season a strength.

In corduroy slacks and a warm sweater, I have walked from my house by the university's horse pastures and across the campus hundreds of times. On the way home, I detour through

Brookside Park. Certainly this is not the most beautiful or impressive park I have ever seen, but it has played a rich role in our family life. When my son was in nursery school, I picked him up and we headed joyfully for the park every nice day. I packed peanut-butter sandwiches and ginger ale; and after our lunch, he ran like a fawn, his chestnut hair touched by sunlight and fresh air. While we went to the park in all seasons, it is in the autumn that my memory tarries. I read or knitted as he climbed on the old red fire engine parked in the same place for half a century now.

The last picnics of the season, on days when your nose got cold and you were happy to return home to a warm fire, were the heartiest. We made them last as long into November as the weather allowed. And that was usually until Thanksgiving weekend. One can almost surely count on a snowstorm in central Iowa as the holiday neared. It is as if the weather responds to the words, "When all is safely gathered in, let the winter storms begin."

One year, though, we were given a reprieve. It was for me the most perfect kind of weather. Frost kept the ground crunching beneath our feet as my son and I headed for his childhood haunt. My mittens were warm, and the wool scarf, tight around my chin, kept the chill away. He was home from college, for the first time appreciating his boyhood from an adult perspective.

"Mom," he said, "places like Ames have to continue to exist, so people will have them to come home to on Thanksgiving."

We were sitting on the running board of that old fire engine, and I responded that I too prayed that time would not change the peace and the pace of life here.

"We'll always have Ames," I said, as I surveyed our "park."

My son could not resist the unconscious echo of *Casablanca* in my phrasing. Without missing a beat, he said, "Here's looking at you, Mom."

We walked home, up the rugged stone steps that led from Brookside to the street above. House after house, street after street, were as familiar to me as my own. A strong arm caressed my shoulder, so different from the little hand I once held tight on our daily journey. We talked so comfortably, I was warmed by our togetherness. I discovered the friendship of my child on that Thanksgiving day, before winter ended my endless autumn.

Her Last Journey

My little boy slipped off her lap. Her arms that had held him tight around the middle opened as he flew away like a butterfly, her hands extending forward as if guiding him. Just a few weeks earlier, my sister had called me, excited that our grandmother had arrived for her visit.

"I looked out my front window, and there she was walking up our long hill," she said in some disbelief. "She was earlier than she had told us, and we weren't expecting her."

But there she was on her own timetable, a woman nearing eighty, clad in a fold-out plastic rain bonnet, making her last journey. She told my sister words my sister had waited years to hear—that her house was as clean and neat as a pin. She stayed as long as she cared to, hugging my sister's four good-bye, and moved on to my house.

Even with Grandma Chapman to help us, my lifestyle was

much more haphazard—but then, my grandmother had come to expect that. She didn't seem to mind the piles of books and stacks of papers. She looked instead at the lace curtains at my windows. "Where did you get such lovely goods?" she asked. When I told her that I had found them through a little ad in the back of a magazine, she seemed amused. But she was more astonished that I could just pop them into the washing machine and have them come out "so nice."

"Not like all our starching and stretching," she reminded me.

These were lovely, I acknowledged, but would never compare with those curtains at our wonderful old house.

It was early fall, and my young one was gone half-days. We had just sent him off to school with a laundry bag of essentials bigger than he was.

"I declare, such goings on," my grandmother said when she saw all his gear. She remembered farther back now, even beyond her own daughter's school days to her own. "All of us went to a one-room schoolhouse," she said once again. "But we learned our lessons."

Oh, how I know, for she had taught me the multiplication tables exactly the rote way she had recited them in that Nebraska school. And she sang me to sleep with tunes like "Bringing in the Sheaves," hardly a lullaby but a song drummed into her as a schoolgirl.

"What will you name a girl?" she had asked me when I was expecting my child. Neither of us had any experience with boys, so this was the logical question to be asked first.

"I love my husband's great-grandmother's name," I confessed to her. She never expected me to use either of her names—they were old-fashioned, she reminded me. She liked the idea of "Jenny" though—Jenny Walton.

"That's a lovely name, Chicken, reminds me of my people, too," she said accommodatingly.

My grandmother's mother and Jenny Walton would have been contemporaries, and if not related by blood, surely sisters of experience. Both were hardworking, God-fearing women; both cooked, cleaned, sewed, and tended to their families with complete devotion. Their husbands were homesteaders and farmers. Both had come west in covered wagons. My grandmother's stories of growing up in Nebraska were so like Aunt Mary's tales of Jenny Walton's Iowa farm life. No wonder my grandmother liked and trusted my husband at first sight—she knew his kin.

Jenny was not born to all of us on that cold November day, however. But my grandmother continued to remind me how partial she was to the name, perhaps hoping one day I would have a girl. I guess I never could quite let it go either. By the time I found the right way to bring Jenny Walton to life, my grandmother was not there to cheer me on. It would have pleased her no end to be in on my little conspiracy. We were always the best at secrets.

We all knew in our hearts that this was probably my grandmother's last journey. Her trip was like an old actress's farewell performance. She saw us all off on our lives, the way she had tucked us into our safe beds. She saw we had ones to love and to love us, and she was satisfied to retire. She would not be strong enough again to hike up that long hill or to return home by train instead of flying, because she wanted "to see more of the country."

"And why do I need to get anywhere so fast?" she insisted.

I called my stepmother to protest. "Talk to her," I pleaded.

"It won't do any good. She'll do as she pleases," she said,

resigned to a lifelong stubborn streak. My stepmother called to let me know my grandmother had arrived safely.

As my grandmother became more and more frail, she covered for her lapses with inimitable charm. On one visit I discovered she had switched from making "real" coffee to stirring in a teaspoon of an instant brand she intentionally mispronounced. "This 'Mixmax' is so much better," she insisted. Perhaps so, but it was easier for her, and she couldn't make a mistake.

She was still walking to the post office near the home she shared with her daughter, often sending me mementos she had always wanted me to have. They became more and more precious. The day came when letters to me were addressed with only our first names—the three of us. "It's friendlier that way," she said—and less trouble.

Those letters are in a small drawer in a walnut rolltop desk from Jenny Walton's Redfield home. I don't look at them very often, but I know just what they say, every word.

My journey has gone on now, years after my grandmother's ended. When Jenny Walton was created to be my heart's voice, it was my grandmother who spanked her into being.

AFTERWORD

AFTERWORD

"There's no use trying," [Alice] said:
"one can't believe impossible things."
"I daresay you haven't had much practice,"
said the Queen. "When I was your age,
I always did it for half-an-hour a day.
Why, sometimes I've believed as many
as six impossible things before breakfast."

—LEWIS CARROLL,
THROUGH THE LOOKING-GLASS

"Your grandmother would be very proud of you," the letter began. The stationery was professional and prestigious, and in the right-hand corner was a name I recognized and the title president beneath it. The letter from this now-president of a prominent insurance company division went on to recall that we were friends from high school. Of course, he would begin by remembering my grandmother's role in my life when he read in the *New York Times* that I was the editor in chief of a new magazine. And he would know how her hopes and dreams for me were being fulfilled just as if she were there to guide my every step. When we talked about it later, he would know, too, that she would worry that I was working too hard, not getting enough rest, and probably not eating right. She would have been right, as usual.

My well-being always came first with my grandmother. When my little son was beginning to show us "how smart he was," I bombarded her with his accomplishments. "Well, why wouldn't he be," she retorted, "with all the attention you have given that boy? If you had had all that at his age. . . ." I came first in her mind, even on the day the friend described above called early in the morning on Russian Orthodox Christmas to wish me good luck.

"In our tradition," he informed my grandmother when she answered the phone, "the first person you talk to has good fortune for the year." To which my practical and protective grandmother responded, "When she gets up, I'll be sure to give her the good luck." This vigilant guardian was not going to disturb my rest.

"Your grandmother" was my friend's first thought after reading the interview with the insightful reporter who earned a prize from me that day, the only one I have to give him, the thanks of a grateful heart. For if he had not pursued his thoughtful line of questioning he would not have hit upon the legacy that I value beyond all else. If he had not mentioned my maiden name, my wonderful letter would not have arrived from someone who was witness to my grandmother's love and inspiration firsthand. How comforting it was and is to have this person from my girlhood in my life still to help me with the memories so few now share. And so *Victoria* magazine, I have often said, was first embraced by women who loved their grandmothers, as I did mine.

Several years before, I had met the man many in the magazine industry consider the master of new-magazine development. As it turned out, his reputation is well deserved. Over a period of several years, he and I had pleasantly discussed ideas for new magazines. One day he asked me to join his company to put those ideas into practice. The one I had tucked in my heart would be the end result of our working together. For the support, confidence, and wisdom he imparted, I shall be forever grateful to him and to all the people in my new company who somehow had the courage and vision to guide me in the way I now believe I was meant to go. With my son just off to college, now was the time to take the chance, to fly on my own wings with years of experience behind me. I left my good job and a host of well-wishing colleagues. So it was with flowers and fond farewells that I left Iowa and came to New York City.

I had been talking for several years about a magazine for women that was different. I had the notion that most of the magazines in the early 1980s were being directed primarily to women's roles. You were either a homemaker *or* a working woman. Naturally, the same woman might be both, as I was, but women were buying their magazines with these motivations. With women going pell-mell into the workforce, I saw no place in the magazine world where women had an opportunity to celebrate their femininity—to celebrate the unique beauty of being a woman. I wanted to talk to women in a different way. I wanted women to feel about a magazine the way my grandmother had always felt about hers. I wanted to create a magazine women would buy with the same kind of passion my grandmother had. A revolutionary, old-fashioned yet contemporary magazine, I thought—a timeless magazine for a trendy era. Geared to the needs of today's woman, it would at the same time be grounded in the things that women had always loved and would always love.

My grandmother and I waited each month for her magazines to arrive. She was a loyal subscriber to at least half a dozen. She would say, "Have you seen my magazine?" The two of us pored over the pages together. Her big black notebooks were taken down from the shelf, and clippings from the magazine, mostly recipe ideas, were pasted in. "I'd like to try this," said this superlative cook of some notion that probably told her to add a can of soup to make her sauce from scratch. Something about her open-mindedness led her to at least entertain the validity of the idea. She loved instant coffee when it first came out, particularly the kind with crystals. Science and convenience were both things she respected while still making her own noodles on Sunday morning. Her desire to keep up with things sometimes found us in Macy's basement for an entire Saturday watching demonstrations of every kind of fry pan and vegetable slicer. I didn't share her passion for the activities, but I loved being with her, and at the end of the day we went to a wonderful restaurant, just the two of us.

When I arrived at my new company, a bouquet of red roses was already on my desk from one of my old friends, bless her, because I was starting from the beginning without a paper clip in sight and was scared to death. I had been fortunate enough to convince two former colleagues to come with me on this new venture. Both had left my former company before me. Married to each other, they had been working on a publication in Colorado but were willing to join me in a venture none of us knew would be successful. In one way or another, they are both still affiliated with the magazine. One never forgets this kind of loyalty, despite the changes that make it necessary for work lives to take different directions. We had one issue to prove ourselves, and we worked like demons with little interference from the company who was backing us. More blessings are bestowed here, because it has been my experience that one seldom gets this kind of freedom in the business world. We were given the assurance that it was our show, and it was a once-in-a-lifetime chance, we thought, as we spent hours together making a magazine as if we were hand-stitching a tapestry.

But the night I saw the first issue coming off the presses in a Maryland printing plant, my stomach sank. The project I had worked on for months, in my control, was now out of my hands. Who would buy this magazine? No one, I thought in terror. What made me think I could do this? Why did I believe anyone would care? I had left a perfectly good job to take on this challenge. My son was in college, tuition had to be paid—what was I doing? It was very lonely at three in the morning with only the machines and a few pressmen as companions. Fortunately for all of us, women understood.

"Dear gentle people, how did you know?" wrote a woman from Birmingham, Michigan.

"I wear business suits to work, I live in a contemporary house, but I am *Victoria* at heart," confessed an advertising executive in another letter.

The letters came day after day and month after month, and the sentiments were in many ways the same. We saw from our correspondents that the emotional concerns of women were being ignored as their own energies and desires drove them into perfecting the roles they had chosen. More and more we found women were forgetting about themselves, about their womanliness, about the ways they had traditionally connected to other women. Some letters even expressed it in just these terms. *Victoria*, they said, was reminding them of the quality of their lives as well as its practicality, of the timelessness of things that never really change, of what was important to pack into their woman's journey. And these were not earthshaking notions we had raised. As one journalist who has written about the magazine observed, we were choosing what was beautiful over what was not, choosing what was life-affirming over what was not. We were choosing to look at the enchantment of childhood, rather than our society's all-consuming preoccupation with the problems of child-rearing.

Make no mistake about it, we would not subtract one moment's concern from solving such problems; we would only add a voice to cherish childhood for its innocence and promise. We were investing home with the importance that it once had and, we hope, can have again as all within strive to make their lives more joyful and peaceful.

Jenny Walton was born with the first issue. In the stories I wrote from my own experiences and those of my family, I integrated my own life with that of the magazine's. And in some ways the morals of my stories, mostly published on the last page of the magazine in the "Chimes" department, meshed with the underlying theme of the magazine. While Jenny would never consciously ignore the problems of life, she saw her role as shining her light on life's positive aspects. While *Victoria* magazine never assumes life is not full of real problems to which real solutions must be sought, it acknowledges that there are many good places to find that kind of information. On its pages there are rewards and affirmations. And so the magazine does not talk from the position of solutions, but it lets its pages unfold as a rosebud unfolds with the flowering of women who share their talents and their inspiration with others.

Every day since *Victoria* began, I have been mindful of the good sense, good cheer, and support of our readers. Sometimes I get to meet them "up close and personal."

When a woman comes to me, whether in a shopping mall or at one of our own events, and takes my hand to tell me with tears in her eyes that the spirit of the magazine helped her get through the death of a child or the chemotherapy following breast-cancer surgery, I am always overcome. We almost always hug each other in an understanding that I cannot put words to. How could a magazine possibly have had such an effect? How can you write a business plan that says people need to know that their values will endure and that we need to preserve and pass on the art of living—and still be taken seriously? Norman Cousins found that humor was healing, and so, apparently, are the meaningful stories and traditions that we preserve generation after generation.

Would my grandmother be proud that they tell me that the magazine has brought them great solace and comfort as well as great pleasure? You bet, but again she might remind them that I work too hard. But, beloved Grandmother, remember I took on the job just as you did when you baked fifty pies in one night for the church supper or sewed for me for days so my dress would be a knockout on the night I met a boyfriend's parents for the first time.

If our pages speak to the beauty of a woman's life through the artfulness of the things she has gathered about her, then we are dealing with intangibles that are not easy to quantify. When our country was settled, our foremothers took with them in those covered wagons moving west a teapot from home, candlesticks that had been in the family, a tablecloth embroidered by a great-grandmother in Europe. Holding on to these reminders of home and family gave them the courage to go on.

Guiding a staff who cares about the content of the magazine as if they were the watchdogs of civilization has had rewards beyond measure. The same connection seems to exist amongst us as it does amongst our readers. No one can work at *Victoria* long without becoming part of "the conspiracy." When someone leaves to become a full-time mother, we stay in touch, giving and receiving assignments between feedings and play dates. We cheer when one of us goes on to fulfill a dream, as a former copy editor is now doing. She will be a pediatrician when she graduates from medical school in another year. And we try to be good to each other in the day-to-day deadline-driven work of putting out a magazine. We are in very many ways a family, with all the attendant joys and sorrows. Most of all, I love them for understanding when I say things I don't mean; when I'm imprudent, and they just don't pay too much attention until I come to my senses. We have come to trust each other in some quite remarkable ways. A dear friend of mine said to me shortly after the magazine came out that it didn't have to be as good as she deemed it to be. She was a former colleague, and she knew the lengths I would go for perfection. She was right in principle. Just don't tell it to anyone on the staff. We make mistakes, but I remind them that if our hearts are in the right place, the readers will understand. So far I've been proven right, and our executive editor is deservedly proud when we hear that English teachers are using our articles in their classes as examples of good contemporary writing.

If *Victoria* bewilders some, perhaps it is because we are in so many ways today cautious of our own emotions and those of others. Not too long ago a colleague confessed to me that *Victoria* had changed her as a person, and she was happy that her life was taking new directions. I wanted to take all the credit for this, but I had to remind her that in these years she had had several children, and motherhood changes us. The tomorrows bring back our yesterdays. Maybe we helped her remember. And maybe we just made it possible for her to express herself in such a way. Sentiment is something we find as frightening as intimacy.

How liberating it is to find there is a place for both.

My grandmother taught me to dream dreams, and I have never ceased to do so, no matter how improbable they have seemed to others at the time. Most improbably, I have found myself sitting down with a former First Lady and her family at a *Victoria* luncheon honoring Lady Bird Johnson for creating the National Wildflower Research Center. I have visited Pretty Penny, the home of Helen Hayes, and interviewed that First Lady of the American stage. I have gone on to produce a staged reading by Julie Harris of Queen Victoria's letters and journals (with the incomparable Richard Kiley as Prince Albert). All of these remarkable women—and now many others—were named by *Victoria* "A Star in Our Crown," but the honor has been all ours in bestowing this award on women who have inspired us by pursuing their own dreams.

The mayor of the City of New York reminded me that the name of the award our magazine was about to give to two women—Edna Lewis, a Southern woman who had worked tirelessly to preserve the traditions of African-American cooking, and Enid Haupt, heiress to a publishing fortune who "gave her jewels to create gardens"—came from an old church hymn. It had come to me from my grandmother.

And so that night, as I had done on one other occasion, I told an audience of dinner guests gathered at a handsome nineteenth-century New York club filled with candlelight and roses brought to full bloom, that I had learned this lesson, along with so many others, sitting by my grandmother's side as we snapped beans or peeled apples: "If you do an unselfish thing, and if you don't expect to be praised for it, you will have a star in your crown," she told me. She had no idea that this belief, planted in me on the back-porch steps, would have such far-reaching implications. I am sure she learned it from her mother on that Nebraska farm where she was reared, or in her church. The river has taken the land where she once lived. The sod houses are now museum pieces.

"Good gracious, child," I can hear her saying at the thought of my fancy notion to carry her plainspoken belief to such lengths. But she did not simply teach me the words, she taught me their meaning in a thousand ways. She must have an entire galaxy of stars in her crown for the acts of love she gave to a child who came into her life a lost seven-year-old.

The award has since been given to a dozen other women whose courage and vision made it possible for us to have a museum for women's art, to see the beauty in vintage laces, to start an aquarium where children can learn the wonder of nature, and to stand on the frontier of medicine—among other noteworthy accomplishments. And I hope it will be given to dozens more over the years. All the recipients will be those who were motivated to do more than anyone could think to ask, to take their dreams to heights many would never believe they could. All would have done these things if there were no rewards.

When I pin on the gold crown with a small diamond chip designed at Tiffany's and present an etched crystal vase, I have my grandmother in my heart, and I see her in my mind's eye, her hands resting in her lap, at peace that the world is in the right place, just as she was when I did an errand for an elderly neighbor or knitted afghan squares for the ladies at the Methodist home.

Lillian Hellman once wrote that she was not old enough to like the past better than the present. Oh, how I agree with her. All of us keep packing our hopes and dreams into our lives alongside the fabric that has been woven from our memories. Not a day goes by when I do not remember, not a day goes by when I do not plan. I hope you, dear reader, have a safe journey and that you are wise in your choices. If this book has helped you to cherish your loved ones, understand your gifts, and listen to your woman's heart, then my beloved grandmother would truly be proud of us all.

NANCY LINDEMEYER is the editor-in-chief of *Victoria* magazine. She lives in Ames, Iowa, and Ardsley-on-Hudson, New York.